Emma's book is a blueprint for achieving whatever you set your mind to. Best of all it actually works! She's the perfect example of how with this very book! It's the ideal read for anyone who needs a helping hand to get their shit done.

Lisa Burling, Business Owner of LBPR
www.lbpr.com.au

A fun, fab book - easy reading and great advice you can easily apply. Reading the book is like sitting down with your girlfriend and she is helping you sort your shit out. Emma is the bomb! Thank you!

Jude Dowsett, Business Owner of Hey Happy Jude
www.heyhappyjude.com.au

If you wanted to use a highlighter to highlight all the thought provoking, inspiring and lightbulb moments you read, you would have a very colourful book indeed!

Whether you want to make a big change or a small change, change lots of things or just one thing; **change** is guaranteed so buckle up and enjoy the ride!

Sharyn P.

I've heard it all before but you have put it in the way I understand. No long stories or paragraphs. Just as a friend telling you the way a friend tells you. Like you say JFDI!

Juanita K.

*Emma's no **BS** attitude to taking control of your life is perfect for those needing an almighty kick up the butt to get into action. Thanks for an entertaining and empowering read.*

Stephanie Meads, Business Owner of Life Wellness Co. www.lifewellnessco.com

…Emmas awesome book has answers to a lot of questions I have not worked out yet, she has helped me along my path…

Csabi Z.

Absolutely love the book! It makes you think about what it is exactly that you want and what shit you need to get done. It also made me realise that I am so much more than I thought I was and that I'm capable of anything I put my mind to. The humour in the book made it great for a laugh too.

Mel E.

Emma has shown us how that by breaking things down into manageable chunks it makes it so much easier to just do it and then you get shit done!

Maiya Kenny, Business Owner of Healing Steps
www.healingsteps.com.au

I've found The 7 secrets to getting Sh*t done absolutely invaluable ! Need help getting up earlier in the morning? Keep it by your bedside and read a couple of pages before bed. Need that extra push to clean out that overflowing wardrobe? Emma is your inner voice guiding you all the way.

It's been my ready reference to stay grounded in times of overwhelm and the best possible no nonsense kick up the butt to finally take action.

Leigh B.

Let me start by saying THANK YOU Emma..... I got my SHIT DONE!! I bought your book and read it in a week…which for me is a FIRST! I can't remember the last time a read a whole book but with yours I couldn't put it down.

Within days I had written and completed my list of things to do. This made me realise how easy it is and how little time it takes to get shit done when you JFDI! I even got focused and sorted out my paperwork to figure out on how to get a new car. Within the week I had bought a car! It was the biggest thing to do on my list.

I can't wait to see how much more I can get done by using your book!! Thanks again!

Stella I.

Emma, I wanted what I say to be really inspiring and meaningful as that is what your book has done for me, in more ways than one. Little by little I am learning to organise and manage my time more efficiently and spend time with my daughter and husband which is so important.

I like to read parts of your book nearly every night as a reminder of how to handle everyday struggles. So thank you and I look forward to your next book!

Sarah L.

Funny…inspiring and to the point!

Elizabeth P.

The 7 secrets to getting shit done

By Emma Queen

Expert in getting shit done

Author, Mentor, Coach & Mum

Copyright 2016 © by Emma Queen

ALL RIGHTS RESERVED. No part of this book may be reproduced or transmitted form by any means, electronic or technical, including photocopying and recording, or by any information storage and retrieval system, except as may be expressively permitted in writing from the publisher.

ISBN: 978-0-9945349-0-3 Paperback Version

ISBN: 978-0-9945349-1-0 eBook Version

This publication is designed to provide accurate and authoritative information in regard to the subject matter covered. Its is sold with the understanding that the publisher is not engaged in rendering legal, accounting or other professional service. If legal advice or other expert assistance is required, the services of a competent professional should be sought.

Book cover, graphics and book designed by Queen's Publishing.
Edited by Matt Houston

Headshot photography by Illawarra Headshots.
Published by Queen's Publishing www.queenspublishing.com.au

Printed in Australia.

First Edition January 2016

Second Edition May 2016

Third edition June 2020

Contents

About the author — 11

Acknowledgments — 13

Pre-Introduction — 15

Break the rules — 16

Actual introduction and the shit you need to read first — 19

The 7 secrets to getting shit done model — 26

Secrets to getting shit done:

Secret #1 - Take Action — 29

Secret #2 - Get Clear — 48

Secret #3 - Your WHY — 58

Secret #4 - Your Identity — 66

Secret #5 - Change your state — 75

Secret #6 - Get Organised — 82

Secret #7 - Set a timer — 100

Bonus Secret - Your Beliefs   104

Food for thought   **107**

Does your brain hurt/Next minute   108

Last minute   114

Care Less   119

I failed   123

Ask for help   127

Near Miss   131

Being scared   134

What are you here for?   137

You are what you say you are   139

Too comfortable with pain   141

Plan A or B   145

Opportunity or Obligation   147

Without Judgement   150

Do you save for 'best'?   153

Say YES	154
Watching or taking part	156
Green & Growing or Ripe & Rotting?	157
Runs in the child	159
I forgive	161
What are you focusing on?	163
Care Even Less	166
Are you a toe dipper?	169
Changing course	171
I said nothing	175
I don't want satisfaction	178
Friend Goals	181
Push it	184
Don't stop believin'	186
Listen here	188
I want to be heard	190

Stop your dreaming	192
Cheering you	194
If you can dream it, you can do it	197
Wheres your choice?	200
Your Commitment	204

About the author

Emma Queen is the expert in getting shit done, a successful author, mentor, coach and mum originally from Birmingham, UK. She has resided in Australia for the last 20+ years.

She has operated and owned several businesses over the last 15+ years and her online business has an international clientele.

Her frank and fresh approach to life ensures she calls her clients on their BS, supports and encourages them…and extracts their awesomeness to create a life they love.

You can join her programs, get coached by her or give her a high-five in the street at anytime. She is a fabulous trainer and speaker to boot.

Her motto is 'Success is found in a place of uncertainty'.

"...I can't recommend Emma enough – she has helped me change my life and I couldn't be happier!..." Kristy

You can contact her via the following channels:

www.emmaqueen.com.au

www.facebook.com/expertingettingshitdone

www.instagram/emma_queen_australia

Email: hello@emmaqueen.com.au

Acknowledgements

In my world I am so very fortunate to have some awesome people around me who keep me real, grounded, challenged, accountable and focused. I love them dearly and of course shit me at times - but it doesn't take away from my love for them.

Funnily enough, they love me back.

Thank you to my soul sisters - you know who you are.

Thank you to the peeps who are happy to answer the phone for a chat, for feedback, advice and love. Again you know who you are.

Thank you to Jude who pulls me up, calls me out on my bull shit and makes me laugh daily.

Thank you to my mum and sister for supporting me even though they have no clue what I get up to most days! *They live in the UK.*

Thank you to my people on social media and in real life. Thank you to my 6am clients, I don't know how you put up with me after all these years...oh that's right! Because you know I am awesome too. ;)

Thank you to my amazing daughter Chloe who lights up my world. She keeps me grounded and the reality checks are helpful. Chloe you will help change the world - I just know it. xx

Thank you to the various coffee shops I have frequented to get this book written - Gwynneville Bakery, The Giddy Goat and Pod. You guys rock!

Lastly, thank you dear reader for picking up this book. I know it will help you in some way - please share the love and pass it onto someone who needs it after you have read it.

Emma xx

Pre-Introduction

I am not even sure if I am allowed to have a pre-introduction on my book? But hey, I am a rule breaker, so here you go!

It's a funny thing writing a book. Or maybe not… *perhaps it's really serious?*

In fact, I came up with a lot of the ideas during a 'float'.

Yes in a floatation tank actually. In the dark, quiet and peace of the tank where my full body was supported by salt water - it came to me. Kinda cool.

I had been writing bits and pieces, ideas on scraps of paper and had thoughts around an actual printed book at some point. I had also been writing daily for just a few weeks and throughly enjoying it.

A woo-woo astrologist had told me several years ago that I was a writer. Piffle! I said at the time. Not a chance. But in the end I was drawn to writing. And this is where I am today. Sometimes you can't deny the pull. You just gotta let it take you to where it's meant to go.

The hilarious thing about writing a book about getting shit done - means you can't really mess around. I had to get my shit done! I had to apply the theory in this book to myself. So the proof is in the pudding my friends! I wrote this book in under 4 weeks. Then got it printed less than 2 weeks later.

I got my shit together and you are reading the finished product.

It is possible.

Break the rules

As you will notice, this book wouldn't pass the English HSC for its 'correct' use of the English language. It's written as I would talk.

I am a rule breaker and I encourage you to break some rules too. *No, I am not referring to speeding on the freeway or anything illegal here.*

I am talking about doing what you want to do - no rules attached.

Go against the grain.
Go against what you are 'supposed' to do.
Go against what people 'think' you should do.

I'll use me as the example here. *I can anyway, as I am the one writing the book.*

'Oh, you need to have a publisher to publish a book'.

'Oh, you need to have a qualification to write a book don't you?'

'Oh Emma, publishing a book is hard work!'

Bloody hell.

No I don't 'need' a publisher to publish a book. But I thought it would be fun to start a publishing house with my bestie.

So I did.

Check it out - the logo is on the cover. Queen's Publishing.

Done.

I do have a stack of qualifications, you know. But not in English, or writing stuff. However I do have a PHD in being awesome and that's all I need hey?

Hard work. Hmmmm…define hard work for me? I don't find it hard doing something that I love. I don't find it hard to sit in a different coffee shop every day for a couple of hours with my laptop. I don't find it hard to use my brain and think about this whole book process in a smart way.

You choose what to believe. All I am saying is re-think your beliefs, break some rules and do 'something'.

This book will help you see/do/feel this.

I know it.

And as my nan said - I can feel it in my waters.

Anyway, on with the show! I mean book…

Actual Introduction and shit you should read before you start this book.

First some questions...

Why are you reading this book?

Do you want to get shit done?

Are you sick of not getting shit done?

Exactly why did you pick up this book?

Now, I'm not complaining, I'm actually quite excited that you've picked the book up because it's my mine for goodness sake!

Why wouldn't I want you to read it?

The fact is - **getting shit done is what I do.** And I do it really well.

In fact...it's what you can do too and I'll teach you.

Sometimes (or all of the time) when we start looking at things we really need to get done...and we don't have the motivation to do it - this is when we get a little stuck. Yep your shit gets stuck (Pun intended!).

Many many people are waiting for motivation to knock them on the head, but it's not about motivation! It's not about waiting for that bump on the head.

Because waiting will get you **nowhere.**

It's about consistency and habits.

So the aim of this book is is to teach you how to get shit done, through habits and other helpful stuff.

This book is designed - so you can pick up a chapter or two and do 'something'. But you can also follow the model on on the next few pages and use it time and time again!

As you will find, it is also a practical book/tool too. So keep on reading my friend...

What are the benefits of **getting** shit done?

What are the benefits of **not** getting it done?

The second question is something to have a good think about.

What are you **gaining** from not getting your shit done?

Whenever we don't do something it can often be linked to something that you gain from not doing it. Sound odd?

Yep it is, but totally true.

I'll give you an example:

Bob really doesn't want to move out of his parents house. He is 30 years old and probably should get his shit together, yes?

But Bob gains so much from staying at home. Yes he gets the obvious stuff - low or no rent, meals cooked for him and his washing done. But what he really gains from not moving out is **taking responsibility for himself.**

It's an easy one, he can blame others for not moving (the Government, his employer for not paying him enough, his parents for being nice... the list will go on..) it's an easy thing to do. **It's easy to blame.**

It's easy to not do something and he gains so much from not moving.

I could go on with more examples but I really want you to start getting your shit done.

I want you to be totally honest with yourself and ask the question:

'What do I gain from **not** getting my shit done?'

I think you will find valuable insights to the reasons why you don't do some shit.

Just sayin'.

So let's keep on track.

A question I get asked all the time is **how do I get so much done?**

I could say that being a Virgo, fast thinker, and altogether superstar is the answer. *Which of course is kind of true...* but let's look at the facts:

- I am a mum of a teen.

- I don't like to call myself a single mum, but I am. I'm a single mum. Unless as a result of this book being published I find a bloke...hello?

- I have a thriving business.

- I run a number of business networking meetings. I have a lot of fun.

- I hang out with my kid a lot.

- I get out to nature most days.

- I have coffee or wine with friends often.

- I exercise.

- I read a lot.

- I listen to music.

- I travel and go on adventures.

I have a great time in my life, but I also get a shit load of stuff done and I am fairly stress free. It's definitely a question I get asked all the time.

This book didn't take that long for me to work out what you wanted to know...because this is stuff that I do day to day. In fact, this book didn't even take more than a few days to plan and just weeks to write as most of it is second nature now.

Did you know you can achieve the same?

So, the reason I've written this book is to help you guys out. *Oh, and also a little test for me to see if I could really get a book out in a very short amount of time.* Not kidding.

So let's ask an important question - **What is shit?**

And you know I am not actually talking about real shit. *I would advise you to go read a medical book on that one if that's your thang'.*

So when I talk about shit it could be anything.

Slight side note: *Thank you Australia for allowing such a word to be used so easily and without offence. Yay!*

It could be your health, your family, your career, your money, your relationships with your partner, your relationships with your kids, your intimate relationships. It could be a relationship with your friends. It could be *any area* of your life.

Throughout the book I'll touch on different areas, however 'shit' is exactly what you define it to be.

Using the book, when I talk about an action or a step - you can apply that to a certain area of your life. It's really up to you.

You could read the book seven times and apply it to seven areas of your life it's that good!

How do you do this?

You pick the book up, and read it. **Or** you pick the book up and open it at a chapter and use that one to make the step to getting your shit done. *Pretty bloody easy I'd say.*

I have even designed an easy to follow model to use at any time on coming right up! So anytime you need a refresher you can apply it to any area of your life.

The first half of the book are the 'Secrets' and the second half are 'Food for Thought' - bits of reading that you can read in a small amount of time to make you 'think'.

Ok - if you can't be bothered to read it, get somebody else to read the book for you… but that's not really the point of getting your shit done because if you're not reading the book how are you going to get your shit done?

By the way, the audio version is now available for purchase. So you lazy bastards will be fine.

Put the kettle on, make a cup of tea…sit down and start with Chapter 1.

If you want background music to listen to whilst reading I have taken the liberty of making a #getshitdone playlist on Spotify for you. Just head over to Spotify and look for #getshitdone and press play.

You're welcome.

The 7 secrets to getting shit done model:

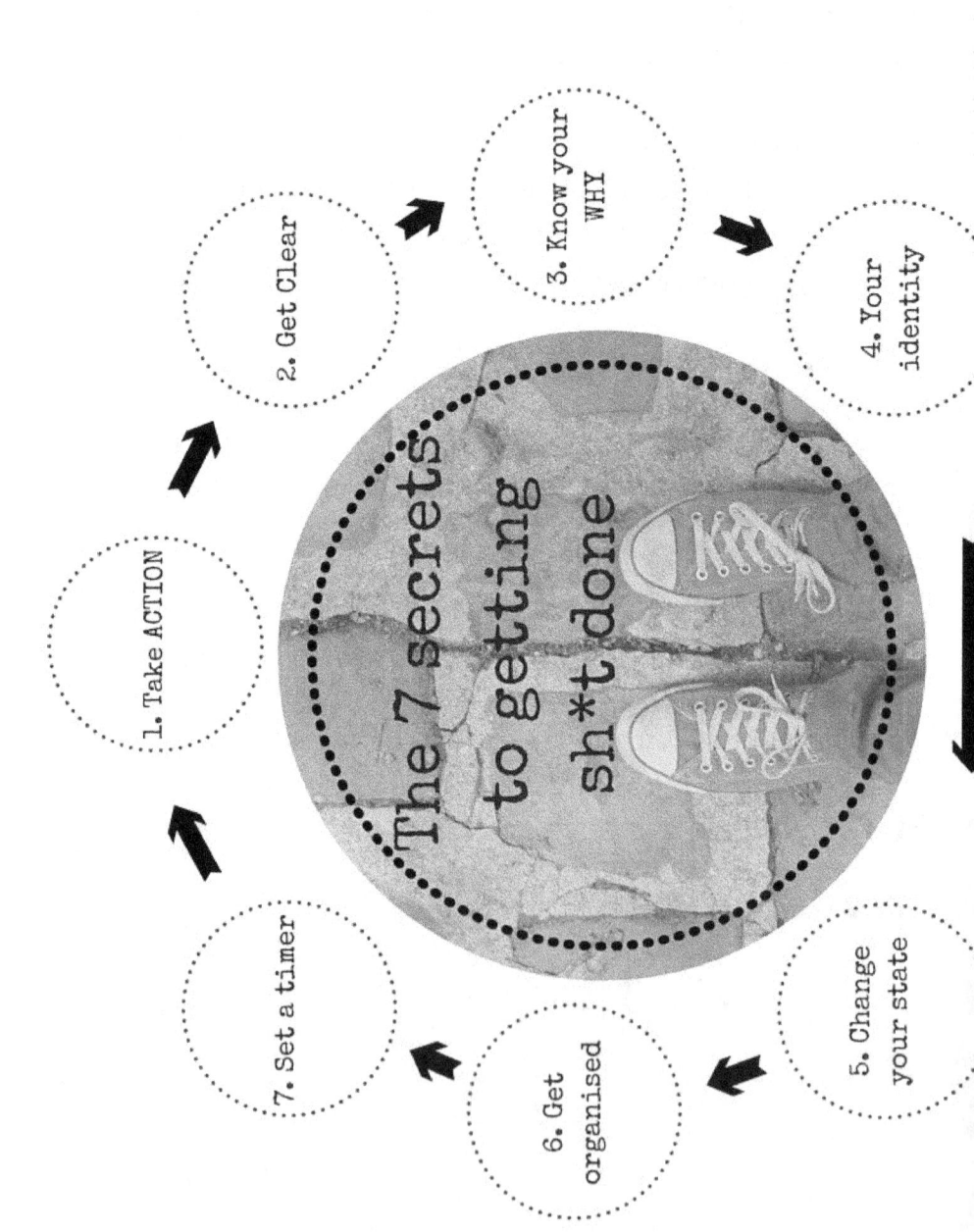

So, the model on the previous page is a simple to follow diagram for whenever you need to get your shit done.

You can simply refer to it at any point - I do suggest that you read the rest of the chapters first though. There is a little more depth to each of the titles.

You can even start at any point on the model and keep going. For example, you could start at number 7 - Set a Timer...then move directly to 1.

Take action.

Does that make sense?

Chapter 1: Secret #1 Taking Action
AKA JFDI chapter
AKA the largest and most important chapter in the book

Even if you read only this one, I would be a happy girl.

Look, the stats on people finishing this book are absolutely ridiculous. 97% of people will not finish a book like this. In fact, only 2% or 3% of people will actually do anything with the information. I want to change these stats, but let's be honest.

Why do you want to take action?

The benefits of taking action mean you move forward in life.

The benefits of taking action mean that you get stuff done, you earn money, you have great relationships, you look after your health blah blah blah. There are so many benefits I am not even going to name them.

You are.

I'm going to get you to write down the benefits of taking action in a moment.

Not only this…you get a sense of achievement or accomplishment to getting your shit done. You want to tell other people about it, and then maybe you could help other people take action as well. Kinda cool huh?

Benefits for me getting my shit done:

....
....
....
....
....
....
....

Use more paper if you need to.

Dictionary.com term

Action

1. The process or state of acting or of being active:

2. something done or performed; act; deed.

3. an act that one consciously wills and that may be characterised by physical or mental activity:

4. actions, habitual or usual acts; conduct: 5. energetic activity:
6. an exertion of power or force:
7. effect or influence:

Gosh who knew? Lots of explanations for that word hey?

Let's have a quick chat about some of the people in the world. If they had not have taken action where would we be today?

The first one that comes to mind is Thomas Edison. He invented the awesome light bulb. (Amongst 1000 other things).

Can you imagine if we didn't have this in our world?

It's crazy, hey?

But did you know he tried 9,999 times to invent it? On the 10,000th go, he achieved it. That's some awesome shit!

That's taking action on a serious level, don't you think? What a dude he is.

Thank you so much, Thomas Edison. You have changed the world. If you hadn't have taken any action, we'd all probably be still living in dark huts looking for scraps on the floor and rubbing two sticks together.

Not my cup of tea, thank you very much.

I could sit here all day harping on about what I learned at history at school of the super cool people that changed our world because they took action, but I'm not going to bore you with that because you can go and Google that yourself.

Actually, I might do that, so check out the back of the book to see if I got that shit done…

To bring it back to the current day, imagine if Mark Zuckerburg had gone, 'No, I'll just smoke some pot while I'm at uni and I will not invent a social network called Facebook.'

No, he took action, and he changed the way we are right now.

This isn't just about Facebook and social media. He helped change the way we communicate today. This isn't about whether you like that or not - it's the way it is. And put it this way, you probably found out about this book on social media anyway.

He took action.

Yes, I know there was a movie, and they said that he didn't invent it and somebody else did. Regardless, whoever it was, they took action, and they changed the world.

Then there's Steve Jobs. (Apple dude who always wore a black turtleneck jumper) He was a pioneer and did, in fact, take action on so many levels that he...again changed our world in so many ways. Yes, yes he was a bit of a dick, but hey he got his shit done!

But don't get me wrong, this isn't about you changing the world or taking action so you can save a million people with your invention. In saying that... it could be...?

What is it about? - it's about you changing your world.

Taking action is about you changing the world that you live in.

To have a more inspired life. To live a creative life. To live a life where you want to live in the world. Where you can teach others or not. To have the money to live a life on your terms. Shall I go on?

Did you know you have a choice in all of this?

When you start taking action, the people around you are also going to take action. It's a little bit magical if you ask me.... but totes true.

So to a side story, you can Google later on if you wish:

Did you know that you're the average of the five people that you hang out with?

That's a little bit of a scary statistic hey? But, it's true.

You're the average of the five people that you hang out with. You're the average age, sex, income, any statistic you want to throw at that...let me repeat for the dummies - you're the average of the people that you hang out with.

This is why a group of single mums will usually all be single mums.

That's why smokers/drinkers will hang around together, why delinquents will hang around together too.

Have a look at the five people around you.

Perhaps ask yourself these questions:

Do they make you feel free or trapped?

They inspire or bore you?

Do they challenge you to grow or shrink?

Do they get happy when you win or lose?

These answers will tell you so much.

Okay - they may be family. I'm not telling you to dump your family and walk off and go and find another five friends. Or maybe do that if they are doing some seriously bad shit?

What I'm saying is recognise who is around you - how can you change it? And are they influencing you in the best possible way?

Are they in fact, action takers? If they're not, okay. You can still love them. Indeed, if they're family...but realise that we do not choose our family. If they are not supporting you or taking you in the direction you want to go in...perhaps, it's time for a think about what to do there.

If they are a friend that's really annoying, walk away. It's okay. We're not at school these days. (If you are at school, find another set of friends that are similar to what you want to be/do/see/have).

If you are at school (or even as an adult!), I highly suggest the following activity.

I had done this exercise with my daughter - age 12 when we did it. If you are a parent...this is a great exercise to do with your kid.

Get a piece of paper and draw an outline of a body. Grab some pens or pencils, and colour works well. Then write what kind of traits you would like in a friend inside that body. Fill the pic up with things you want in friendships - go outside the body if you like. (See picture coming up).

You can get quite creative with this if you like.

Let them fill it in until they can't think of anything else to add.

Get them to look at the picture or list of traits.

Get them to REALLY look at it - and think about the things they have listed.

Then ask them (or you) who this reminds them of?

I think you will find that it's actually them that they have drawn.

They have put the things on there that they are.

The photo on this next page is the actual drawing we did together at the coffee shop.

It's a quite powerful exercise to do! Try it!

Anyway - back to your five people.

You can change your five people around you by other things like books, by using YouTube, by using social media and lifting your average.

It's pretty cool that we have these kinds of resources these days - they can be used for good! Most days I start my mornings listening to inspirational audio or video via the internet. I thank the Universe daily for high-speed internet, you know…

Here is something that helps me; It has always been my intention to be the most unintelligent person in a room because therefore I can learn from that. Quoting Yazz, the only way is up…yes?

Back to you, who are the five people that you're hanging out with/or influences you?

If you want to move up in your career or if you're going to increase your health or improve your relationships, who are the people around you?

Be brutally honest.

I'll give you an example:

Are the people you hang out with, overweight, poor or unmotivated? I am not just talking about your family… you do know that you spend more time with people at your workplace? What are they like? Do they have morning-teas regularly choc-full of chocolate cake and sweet things? Are you eating that stuff to 'fit in'? Or are you eating it not even thinking about it? Because it's a habit? Then do you sit on your bum all day in an office job, drive home on your bum in your car. Go home, watch TV on your bum all night?

Are you starting to understand?

Another example:

If you are on government benefits (for whatever reason) are you spending time with other people on benefits? Don't get me wrong - I have nothing against this...I have been on them myself. But can you see your average is likely to be the same as them? How could you improve this?

Start hanging out with people who have jobs or businesses. You will get inspired to take action, move forward and increase your average.

So, improving your situation - Who could you model off to improve this? If the people around you are all getting divorced, maybe it's time to look at people who are happily married. What are they doing? How would you mimic that? It's not copying, it's called, and I talk about that a bit more on chapter 2.

I'm saying lift your average.

How could you do that?

I've already mentioned it - books, YouTube, motivational speakers, courses...I'm sure you can think of more things yourself…there are so many ways.

The bottom line is that you are a product of who you hang out with. So how do you take action?

It's quite simple.

JFDI.

Just fucking do it.

Or for those people who are not keen on swear words, just freaking do it or just flipping do it.

I don't care what you use; it's a JFDI moment.

The secret to taking action is **taking fucking action.**

I'll even make it way more obvious for you:

The secret to taking action is taking fucking action.

This is not even a secret. We're looking for the magic pill.

However, it is just fucking doing it!

Gosh, it makes me so frustrated. Can you tell?

Make the decision and take action.

It's like saying there's no truck...there's no truck...there's no truck... and pretending that there isn't a problem. Unless you take action by stepping away from the truck or out of the truck's path, then you're going to get hit by the truck. Yes?

Okay, remove truck analogies out of your brain. It's a little depressing. I get it.

There are no weeds in my gardens... there are no weeds in my garden... there are no weeds in my garden.

Unless you take ACTION - there are going to be weeds in your garden.

You're in denial.

It's all about taking action.

A secret to getting your shit done is to JFDI.

Take the step.

Make a move.

If it doesn't work, come back to it and tweak it.

Let's go back to Mr. Edison. 9,999 times of persevering to invent the light bulb. He is quoted when answering questions on his failures as *'I have not failed. I have just found 9,999 ways that do not work'.*

Obviously, it didn't work the first time, so then he tweaked it. It didn't work the second time, so he tried something else. It didn't work the third time, so he tried something else. And so on...

This is where us lowly humans will just give up.

'Oh, I tried everything.'

Have you really?

Have you really tried everything?

Tweak it, tweak it, tweak it.

Tweak the step.

Tweak the step until you get it done.

JFDI.

Take action.

Push through it.

Do it again.

And again.

If it helps, keep reading this book! Because it's going to give you another six ways of getting your shit done.

Certainly, turn to chapter 3 on your why. That one is super important.

Look at an area of your life or the task that you need to do and just fucking do it.

All right?

Yes, yes, there'll be that voice in your head going *'Oh, I don't think you should, or I don't think it's possible'* and then all the naysayers of course.

Actually let me talk about the naysayers AKA the people in your life.

It is possible that they will kick up a fuss. They will make a noise. They will give you their 2 cents. They will provide 'help' loosely termed as 'no help' at all, as it's *their* limitations in life.

Ever heard of the term - *a dog barks at things they don't understand?*

Okay, okay, I am not saying that your family are dogs. You get me here don't you?

The point I am making is that they will probably make a noise - because they think you will change.

They think you will change so much that you won't love them. Well, that's their simplified version anyway. But I think you understand what I'm describing.

Hey, this is your life dude. Why don't you just fucking do it and give it a go?

If we're looking about your health and you're all *'Oh, I've got a knee injury and a sore back.'* Honestly, working in the health field, I've heard it all.

There are people out in this world who don't even have legs, and they can exercise. You and with your little sore knee, you can get out there and go to the swimming pool and start moving. Find something you can do, stop focusing on what you can't do.

It's taking action, moving forward towards a goal.

Taking action a bit at a time.

'Oh, my boss won't give me the promotion.' Well, fuck that!

Go and get some extra training or go to college or teach some into yourself. Get a book, listen to an audio. Learn something, step up, take action and move through it. You never know what might happen.

Don't just sit there waiting for life to take over when you can have control because you are taking action.

Remember to JFDI.

Okay, so I've been a little tough on the first chapter, hey? I apologise if I come over a little 'ranty,' but sometimes you gotta be tough.

What did you learn? It's just about taking a step. Isn't it?

So use this opportunity right now to get started.

Use this book and these pages to answer some questions.

Remember you can use this in any area of your life.

Have a think...what have you done or haven't done in the past?

I **have not** taken this action:

....
....
....
....
....
....
....

I **have** taken this action:

....
....
....
....
....
....
....

What did it take for you to **take action?** What happened?

....
....
....
....
....
....
....
....

What regrets do you have for **not taking** action?

....
....
....
....
....
....
....

What **opportunities** did you miss?

....
....
....
....
....
....
....

What relationships did you miss or not have - as a result of you sitting back and not taking action?

....
....
....
....
....
....
....

What are you going to do **right now?**

....
....
....
....
....
....
....

Right now, what would happen if you *didn't do anything?*

....
....
....

....
....
....
....

What **JFDI** step are you going to make?

....
....
....
....
....
....
....

Use more paper if you need to.

I really recommend - that you have got to keep reading this book because there's a little bit more to these secrets than just doing one step.

Put that kettle back on, and we're off to chapter 2.

If you would like to, you can share this on social media with:

#ActionJFDI
#7SecretsGetShitDone

Good luck.

Chapter 2: Secret #2 Get clear AKA Get some glasses

This chapter is about *getting clear on what your shit is.*

Are you going to be focusing on your family or your career? Or your business... your relationships or your health...or your kids?

What is it exactly?

It could be even your car. It could be an item. It could be a move across the world.

Whatever it is, work out firstly what your shit is.

Because unless you know and you get clear on what it is, **how are you going to achieve it?**

Grab that pen and paper or write below. Write down exactly what your shit is.

My 'shit' is:

....
....
....
....
....
....

Now, let's take a moment to visualise precisely what you want to achieve.

The power of the brain is immense. Go and study up on Neuro-Linguistic Programming (NLP) or type in neuroscience and you'll find that our minds are genuinely magnificent objects.

Our brains know no difference from real and pretend. Our minds will get scared when we watch a scary movie because it simply doesn't know any different. Isn't that true? Your imagination is pretty active, you know. It's way more powerful than you think.

Side note: our brains have the electric consistency of jelly. Weird huh?

Okay, let's get back to the benefit of getting clear on what your shit is.

It means you can go and do it.

So many people in this life say 'Oh, I want to get X amount of money' - but if you ask them how much money that is..they don't know!

....or 'I want to be rich.'

Well, how much is that? My 'rich' is different from your 'rich' - so how much money is 'rich'?

They can often say 'I want to win the lottery.' Some of these people don't even buy bloody tickets!

They're not very clear on what they want, so how are they going to achieve it?

I believe that unless you can language something, you can't have it.

This is exactly what this chapter is about: getting clear on what you want or what you need.

It's not about putting something out there and being limited by our thinking or limited by somebody else's thinking.

This is your life. You get to decide. You get to drive the bus.

Let's get back to visualisation. Close your eyes and take a deep breath.

Obviously, you're reading this book, so just put it to the side one moment after you've read this little bit.

Imagine what it is, that you want to achieve.

Imagine what you'll see, what you'll hear.

If it's an item, what would it feel like?...also what it will sound like?

Is there a smell? Is there a taste? What is there?

Use all of your senses.

It could be a success, but what does success mean to you?

We're not talking about other people here. What does success mean to you?

It could be the dream body. What does that body look like to you?

Visualise it in your mind and embody your imagination...trick that funny little brain of yours into thinking it's precisely there right now.

Because isn't it funny that we can always achieve something if we imagine it to be?

Yes, I know some people believe they haven't got an extraordinary imagination, but if they practice (because we all have the capability), then they will get there. Give it a go!

What have you got to lose?

Now, this is where the magic happens.

Imagine what that goal or action is.

As I've said, write it down and visualise what it would feel like to have achieved that...whether that be next week...tomorrow...in the next hour...next year, in ten years or twenty years.

I don't care when it is but imagine and trick that brain into believing you've already achieved it.

Now, here's the trick. *AKA the hard bit.*

When you get clear on what you want - you have to revisit this often.

If it's a goal that you want to achieve - your ultimate health or your ultimate strong body, or whatever that is. You need to revisit that visualisation daily.

Did you know that athletes regular visualise themselves winning? It's part of their training. Google that shit baby!

Okay, I have an idea.

Perhaps when you do your daily routines*...and us humans love our habits don't we?

*A routine is an action or behaviour that you perform often

Maybe the ritual of making your cup of tea in the morning or perhaps brushing your teeth...or when you are in the shower.

Imagine what it feels like to have achieved that goal or when you are doing that task.

Do this every day.

Do it twice a day for goodness sake if you really, really, really want it.

So brush your teeth...in your head, then imagine your goal/achievement. What it feels like, *what you will see and hear.*

Be in that moment.

You can't tell me that you don't have the time to dream.

You know how to brush your teeth (I hope) - you don't have to think about that.

JFDI.

Okay, so you have to revisit it regularly to start achieving it.

What? Look at your dreams or goals daily? Twice daily? Jeez getting shit done is looking hard...is it?

Is it really hard to spend 6 minutes a day focusing on what you want in life?

If you're a person that likes to write things down, then maybe write it down and have it in front of you as a reminder in the car as you're driving to work. (Please watch the road!) Or if you're more of an auditory person, put it on a recording of yourself talking to yourself.

Example:

Say *'Hey *insert your name here* - Imagine what it feels like to have the ultimate body. Imagine what it feels like to feel lighter, feel stronger and more flexible. Imagine what you would see in the mirror: what clothes would you wear? What would your friends say? What are you hearing?'.*

As you can see, using all of your senses - certainly the main one you use **will** be very effective.

Another helpful hint is to perhaps take yourself to a time where you had already achieved that goal.

Maybe it's something that you've already done in the past.

How did that feel? Go back to that time - what did you do, what did you see, how did you feel?

You know what? **Success leaves clues**, so maybe look at what you did and repeat those steps.

For those of you who have never achieved the thing that you're aiming for, it's totes ok.

Because guess what? Lots of people in this world have already done what you want. I can guarantee it. There's probably someone out there who's either done it or done something similar. They may have even written a book on it. Go find it!

How lucky are we that we have the glorious internet these days? You can find a book on Amazon and download it within seconds - then read it.

This is called modeling in NLP.

Looking at what somebody else has done and model that behaviour.

You may not model every single step that they have done...and no, no, no, it's not copying!

Get over that one. Why reinvent the wheel? Why try and do something that somebody's already done? Take the shortcuts.

It's not cheating; please get rid of that belief. It's not helping you.

For goodness sake, do you think I'm writing this book because I just decided to write a book? Nope.

I've looked at people who have already written books and researched how they did that. Plus if I've met somebody who's written a book, I have asked them how they did it.

Ask better questions.

Rightio - to review this, what is the goal or dream?

Have you gotten clear?

Have you visualised it?

Are you visiting this goal every day or every week? Put it in your diary if you need to. Or use your phone and set reminders.

Get clear on what it is and then maybe...if somebody has already done it, model what they have done.

If, in the instance that there isn't anybody that you can model off because maybe you're a trailblazer - think about documenting those steps or remembering them so you can then teach another person so they can role model off you. *Don't keep it a secret - help others.*

Have a look in the past at what you've achieved. Have you ever been really clear on a goal that you've just gone and done it?

Remember back to chapter one, JFDI. You were probably so clear on it that you just did JFDI...didn't you?

Again, *success will leave clues.* What was it that you did to achieve that? Then repeat.

Sorry to break it to you. But if you're not clear on what you want to do, you will not get there. It is plain and simple.

Having some vague idea about what you want in the future in any area of your life means you probably won't get it.

I'm sorry (not really) to give you the bad news, but guess what? You're reading this book, which means that you're ready to take some action...which means you're ready to get clear on those goals.

Hey, it may not happen instantly.

It may happen when you wake up one morning.

It may happen as you're driving to work one day.

It may happen when you've overheard somebody say something, and that will trigger you into getting clear about what you really, really want.

But it will happen when you are ready.

Or not. Isn't life amazing?

Off you go.

Go and create your dreams and goals.

Not only are you JFDIing it now, but you're also getting clear on it...which takes you that step closer. Maybe that's all you need to do.

Taking action? Get accountable - and share this chapter on social media with:

#Imgettingclear
#7SecretsGetShitDone

Good luck and I'll see you in chapter three.

Chapter 3: Secret #3 Your WHY
AKA Without this chapter you will probably fail

Okay - I'm just warning you.

I could get fairly passionate about this chapter. In fact, if I could have another chapter one I would have - it's that fucking important!

Your WHY.

Having your *why*, your big juicy *why* you need to get your shit done is super-duper-duper important!

Why is it so important?

Well, if you didn't have a *why* then you wouldn't get it done.

Simple.

In my biz, I talk to a lot of people about their reasons why...certainly in the health arena.

For example, why do they need to lose weight?

If it's just to fit into a pair of jeans, hey could buy another pair, and there you go - their *why* is already fixed. Easy. But...their *why* needs to be really, really, really juicy.

'Oh, but why does my why need to be really juicy?' I hear you ask…?

Referring to chapter 6 using the SMARTE goals - the E for *emotion* is vital.

Why do you need to lose weight?

Why do you need to look after your relationships?

Why do you need to change jobs/career/start a business?

Whatever area you are looking at - you need a why.

Why do you need to do this thing, to get your shit done?

Fact: Without an excellent reason why you are not going to get it done. *You will fail.*

Have a look at anything that you've tried in the past and think…'Well, *why didn't I achieve that?'*

It's probably to do with your *why.*

Ok, I get it, you are probably sick of me using the word *why* by now, but really…what other word could I use that would be effective?

Admittedly I have said it enough now for it to stick in your brain hey?

The goal or plan you set (that didn't work) it wasn't juicy enough, it wasn't compelling enough.

Horny.

Ok, that got your attention, didn't it?

I want you to be horny for your why.

You get what I mean when I say horny? Yes?

When you are horny, you go and get it...don't you?

You need to be so, so horny for your why!

Your why needs to be so horny that you are just going to go for it.

Which goes back to JFDI (need I remind you what that means again?).

If a goal is compelling enough - you will just do it.

If you need to make a plan for that, that's cool. If you need to get clear on it, that's cool as well. Use this book to get you horny for your goal!

Having a really juicy, juicy, juicy reason why you are doing something is perhaps one of the most important things to getting your shit done.

Have a think about that one.

I'll give you an example to help you out:

I know a heap of people who want to leave their full-time employment to start a business. They are sick of the restrictions of their job, sick of their boss or want flexibility for their family. I do suggest to them, that they should have a transition plan to move out of their job into their business.

I also know people who work in their full-time job and have had their business on the side for many, many years. They haven't made the 'jump' yet - because they're either too scared or their why isn't big enough.

But I know if something happened to their job...for example, if they got made redundant and they had to finish employment, they would push themselves to make their business work. Because now they have a *why*. They have to feed their family, pay the mortgage and pay for their lifestyle. That's a fairly big *why* isn't it?

A friend of mine, Brad Burton (Founder of 4Networking) has written several books, and he always says that if you've got a plan B, then plan A is not going to work, and I absolutely agree with him.

I'm a big believer in 'burning your boats.' You might have heard/seen stories/movies of people getting to an island and fighting in a war. They burn their boats at the shore and fight harder as they have no choice. Because they have no way of getting back.

Metaphorically for me, that works.

For you, it probably works too. But do we have to be as drastic as burning our boats? Not really...but we have to have such a big, juicy reason why we have to achieve something, otherwise we're just going to sit back and take the easy road.

Have you ever burnt your boats somewhere in your life? What happened?

Did you fight that bit harder?

Think about that for a moment.

A bit on your comfort zone

Do you step outside of your comfort zone much?

I'll agree, it's comfy in there...but are you expanding this zone at all?

Is setting a goal or plan pushing you outside of this?

I hope so.

Because you and I know that when you do - you learn something, you learn something about yourself or the situation.

When you push through to the other side, what happens then

Another thing, shit happens.

You can fail at things too.

Did you know that there's no such thing as failure, only feedback?

In the past when you have failed at a task or goal, what did you learn?

Other questions you may want to ask yourself:

* Are you taking the safe road?
* Are you taking the easy way out?
* Why are you doing this?
* What is the worst that could happen if you 'stepped out'?

A person I know says '...*that when the worst happens, when the walls come tumbling down, or when my back is against the wall - the best in me comes out.*'

I don't always agree with this saying but to be quite honest; it has worked on occasions.

When the worst has happened, I've gotten very resourceful because my why has gotten very strong. *What about you?*

When the worst shit has happened, I've worked out other ways to do things.

I'm not talking about wars or bankruptcy or anything awful like that. It could be anything, but sometimes when the yucky things happen - you're more compelled to work towards your goal.

I think you'd agree.

Working in the health arena, I get a lot of people come to me who have had a diagnosis of diabetes or a heart condition. And now they need to clean up their diet and start moving. Their *why* has gotten even stronger. It could potentially be life or death, and for most of my clients they are parents, and they want to be around for their kids. So their *why* is massive at this point. I'm sure you can imagine other reasons too as to why they need to sort their health out.

Can you think of an area in your life that you have no other choice but to improve?

It could be money.

It could be where you live.

It could be your relationship.

What could that be and is it juicy enough for you to take some action?

Is it juicy enough for you to get clear...JFDI...make a plan...and get organised?

So what is your *why*?

How can you be horny for it?

What would make the goal or plan compelling for you? Use the next page to work on this now.

My goal/plan:

....

My WHY

....
....
....
....
....
....
....
....
....
....
....
....

For this chapter use the following hashtags on social media to share what you are doing:

#mywhyishorny

#7SecretsGetShitDone

Chapter 4: Secret #4 Your identity

AKA Who are you?

I have a story for you before I start on this chapter:

There was an orphaned girl from Sierra Leone who was just four years old when she was adopted into a family of eleven in the US. She decided that she wanted to be a ballerina after seeing a tattered magazine cover in the street.

She formed an identity around being a prima ballerina. Her mother enrolled her into classes, and she acted like a ballerina - training for hours at a time, her diet, her attitude, her focus. She didn't fit the stereotype of a ballerina though. But that didn't stop her.

By age 14 she won a scholarship for the American Ballet Theatre in New York. Her identity around being a prima ballerina ensured she achieved her goal and now she is one of the few ballerinas at her level, and she currently resides in Amsterdam. Her ultimate dream is to open a ballet school in Sierra Leone. I have no doubt she will achieve this. Her name is Michaela DePrince if you want to read her memoir.

So my friend, who are you being to get your shit done? A secret to getting your shit done is about **your identity.**

Why? Because it's fucking important!

Who are you **being** today to get your shit done?

I know the identity of being an 'entrepreneur'...laying in bed pressing 'snooze' is **not** what they do. So I make a conscious decision (because one of my identities, is of an entrepreneur) that I get up and I move!

Entrepreneurs are healthy. Entrepreneurs take action, so that is what I do. Writing this book is part of those actions right now too.

Think about what your identity is right now. *And yes, you could have a few of them.*

I'll help you out, using me as an example. My identities are mum, business owner, coach, writer, and cleaner. I probably have more, but you get the picture, yes?

To help you out on this theory, a great thing that I've used over the years is the 'Be, Do, Have' model.

It is based on the fact that we often focus on the 'having' of things/ experiences/results etc.

In life, you do not have to **do** anything. It's all a question of what you are **being.**

I first learned this concept in the Neal Donald Walsch book 'Conversations With God.'

Now I am not religious at all…(It's not a religious book anyway) But it is a fascinating read. I do recommend it.

To explain this concept, here is an excerpt. If it's too much, I get it…just skim over to the next bit:

Most people believe if they "have" a thing (more time, money, love -- whatever), then they can finally "do" a thing (write a book, take up a hobby, go on vacation, buy a home, undertake a relationship), which will allow them to "be" a thing (happy, peaceful, content, or in love). In actuality, they are reversing the Be-Do-Have paradigm. In the universe, as it really is (as opposed to how you think it is), "havingness" does not produce "beingness," but the other way around.

First you "be" the thing called "happy" (or "knowing," or "wise," or "compassionate," or whatever), then you start "doing" things from this place of beingness -- and soon you discover that what you are doing winds up bringing you the things you've always wanted to "have."

The way to set this creative process (and that's what this is...the process of creation) into motion is to look at what it is you want to "have," ask yourself what you think you would "be" if you "had" that, then go right straight to being.

In this way, you reverse the way you've been using the Be-Do-Have paradigm -- in actuality, set it right -- and work with, rather than against, the creative power of the universe.

Here is a short way of stating this principle:

In life, you do not have to do anything. It's all a question of what you are being.

*Credit to Neal Donald Walsch

Quite a concept yes?

So, who are you being?

What are you doing to have what you need or to get the results you are looking for?

It's quite a simple one when you process it in your mind.

Even if you applied just this principle to your life, it would change for the better.

Be. Do. Have.

I have these words taped to the inside of my shower, so when I wash my hair, I think about who I am **being**, what am I **doing** to **have** what I want.

Cool hey?

So the *being* bit - is about your identity. I'll help you out with some examples:

If you aim to be a manager in your organisation with twenty-five people under you, what is the identity of a manager who leads people?

What does a manager do? What would their identity be?

Who are they being?

If you don't know what they do or how they are being. Why not ask someone in a similar position? I covered modeling in chapter 2. You could read a book, watch a YouTube video on leadership to help you out and even take a course on it.

Does a manager who leads twenty-five people look after themselves? Does this person continually improve their communication skills?

Start asking better questions.

Who are you *being* to be that healthy person?

Is that healthy person going to order a pizza every night? No.

A healthy person will have smoothies. They'll take classes. They'll learn about their body. They may read information to help them become the identity of a healthy person.

Another example, again…using myself because hey! I'm the author of this book…

…is a writer.

I am a writer.

What do writers do? Writers get up and work. Writers get up and write shit loads of words. Writers burn the candle at both ends, or do they?

No. In fact, I've changed that one because I want to be a writer who doesn't stay up late because I like getting up early!

So question your own beliefs too!

Being a writer means that I need to take care of my punctuation and grammar, while also allowing my personality to shine through. Being a writer means that I am disciplined. I have a plan. I'm organised. I have a diary. I set a timer. This is precisely what I've done to finish this book!

Getting your shit done is attached to your identity.

True dat.

Look at who your identity is here and get that shit done!

What identity do you have around the area of your life that you wish to conquer?

Use the chart on this page to work out which area of your life and what identity you're playing in that. Remember to stop and question what you believe around each identity - just because you think it, doesn't mean it's true.

P.S There is a bit on beliefs in the bonus secret...so keep reading.

Please use the blank spaces for your own areas.

Area of your life	Identities
Health	
Career/Business	
Relationship - Intimate	
Relationship - Family/Friends	
Spirituality	
Finance	

Again in which area of your life are you having a different identity?

By the way, it's totally okay to have 5 or more identities around every area of your life.

Who are you *being*?

What are you *doing*, and what results are you *having*?

Be, do, have everything. That is one guaranteed way of getting your shit done.

Even if you have not yet looked at any other chapter in this book - this shit works!

So grab your pen and paper, and write down who you're being.

Can you model people? Yes, you can. I've mentioned this already - go back to chapter 2 and look at the modeling section.

My identity

Who am I **being?**

....
....
....
....
....

What am I **doing?**

....
....
....
....
....

What do I want to **have?** Or what results do I **want?**

....
....
....
....
....

Who can you be like?

A great question to wake up every morning is:

Who am I going to be today?

You gotta share the following hashtags on social media don't you?

#bedohave

#whatismyidentity

#7SecretsGetShitDone

Chapter 5: Secret #5 Change your state AKA get outta that funk

I'll thank my good old friend Tony Robbins for this one - it's a life changer! Yes, I'll say he's a good old friend because I've seen him several times over the years...Tony talks a lot about state.

Check out the picture below – credits to Tony Robbins.

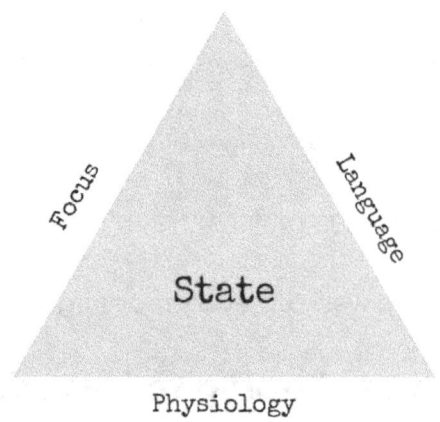

Changing your state can change so many things.

Imagine that you are sitting in your chair (you might be doing it now anyway). And you are looking at your navel...thinking 'Oh, I've got to go and do this, and I've got to do that...' is not motivating, is it?

However...if you chuck on a song and have a boogie in your lounge room, or office...you're a little bit more motivated to do something aren't you?

This is an easy way of explaining your state.

The key is to change the state from where you are...to one that will get more shit done.

Firstly -recognise what your state is.

What is your **language**?

What language are you using in this current state?

You could be speaking or even 'thinking' these things.

Is it things like *'Oh, I'm tired. I was up late last night. I'm feeling sluggish. *Insert negative shit here...'*?

Or *'Wow I feel amazing, what a great day…let's get outside and do something!'*?

Listen and take notice of what you are saying, even to yourself.

Then look at your **physiology.**

Are you sitting slumped over? Shoulders down and your eyes are looking to your feet? Or are you sitting up straight, eyes focused? Are you breathing? Full breaths or barely breathing

Lastly, where is your **focus**?

What are you focusing on? The bad stuff? The stuff you have zero control over? Are you focusing on the good stuff? The potential? The feeling of how you feel when you have finished something?

This is all part of this triangle that my friend Tony put together. I wouldn't try just changing one of these things - they are not sufficient enough.

Change all three.

So how do you change the negative stuff?

It's simple - do the opposite. Or something different.

Change your language.

Change your physiology.

Change your Focus.

I said it was simple; I didn't say it was easy. But it is possible.

Okay, I lied. *Sometimes it is easy.*

Language:

'Oh, I'm energised. I'm excited. I'm invigorated.' Say words that inspire or motivate you.

Your physiology, okay…rather than sitting down, stand up!

Have a dance around.

Get out your car and run around it. (Please ensure that your vehicle has stopped before trying this one).

Do something.

I'm a massive fan of making a playlist to get me motivated to change my state. You can do this easily with iTunes and Spotify.

In fact, I have even helped you out on this.

If you have Spotify (Google it if you haven't) and look for a playlist called #getshitdone. I made you a playlist for those 'moments' when you need to be motivated to move!

You're welcome.

So where is your focus? Go back to chapter 2. Is your action clear? Then look at your WHY - why you're doing this - chapter 3.

Remember to do all three things.

My friend, it's super easy to sit on the lounge and twiddle your life away, but changing your state really does mean you get more shit done! I dare you to try it.

It is one of the key things that I have done for many, many years. *Thanks, Tony I appreciate it.*

So this is about changing your state, so do what you need to do.

If music is your thing, use music. If going for a walk is your thing, go for a walk.

I know going back to nature for me works.

Looking at the ocean, listening to the ocean...even jumping into the sea is a change of state. Use what you have. Even if you only have a patch of grass you can stand on - take your shoes off and feel the grass between your toes and use your fantastic imagination. You can do this!

It's certainly better than sitting in that space of being unmotivated, uninspired and generally yuck.

Talk to someone if you need to. Talk about stuff. Talk to your partner or a friend about a life goal.

Listen to your language and look at your focus too.

All state changers.

Try throwing a glass of water over your own face if you need to. Trust me it works! (I have done it.)

There are so many ways of changing your state. Honestly, it's a super duper secret to getting your shit done.

For this chapter, you must share the following hashtags on social media!

#changingstatenow

#7SecretsGetShitDone

If you do what you've always done.

You'll get what you've always gotten.

Tony Robbins

Chapter 6: Secret #6 Get Organised
AKA De-Clutter and get your shit together or Making a plan

Do you like stationary? I suppose not everyone does, but I am a massive fan of diaries. I'm a huge fan of paper and pens and wall planners and getting it all out on paper…from out of your head.

Onto a whiteboard or onto sticky notes, or whatever you need to do. I'm known to use chalk pens all over my windows when I am brainstorming ideas too.

Secret #6 of getting your shit done is *making a plan or getting organised.*

If you don't like this, tough! It works, so why not give it a go?

If your house is messy and disorganised, *clean it up.*

It's all a matter of energy. Energy cannot flow with things blocking it. Now I may or may not be talking woo-woo, and quite frankly I do not care if I am. But I know this for a fact.

You clear up your shit - good things come back.

Try it. I double-dare you.

I'm not going to talk about decluttering your house. There are a heap of other books out there that talk about decluttering your house/stuff so read one of those, if this is an issue for you.

But I know for a fact that every time I clean a kitchen drawer out - I get something done somewhere else in my life. *Weird huh?*

Maybe it's the secret to the universe? *Who knows…?*

You know how you feel after you've cleaned that linen cupboard out or after you've cleaned out the glovebox in your car...don't you?

Perhaps it's just me? In any case, I don't care what it is.

Top tip: If you don't know what to get organised with - do something. Anything! Even 2 mins spent on cleaning out your wallet or purse feels good, yes?

Again, it's JFDI.

I remember a story about a woman who had piles and piles of paperwork around her house, and she didn't know what to do. Her coach told her to put a tea light candle on every collection of paperwork in her whole house. Now I don't personally recommend this because you could potentially set fire to your home...but she asked the piles of paper what she wanted to do with it (true story) and they said to put it in a book. So she did. She wrote a bestselling book. Who knew? And no, if you were wondering, it wasn't me...haha.

There are weird things that you can do or not so weird things that you could do to get organised.

This is going to work for you, so give it a go. You know that you will feel a whole lot better once you get started.

Now I'm not just talking about getting organised in your house.

This could be your work desk. This could be wherever you spend time in - your car, kitchen or locker.

You cannot get your shit done if you are disorganised. Why? Because your focus is with the shit, you need to clean up, and the energy isn't there even if you are not aware of it.

Now there's no point in harping on to me that you are just one of those people who has a messy house.

Let's delve a bit deeper - why is this so?

It's just the way I am. It's always been this way. I can't change. My family/ pets/*insert excuse here...mess it up.

Is being disorganised part of who you are? Part of your identity?

Maybe it's time to let go of that piece of your identity? Perhaps a new bit could be the more organised version of you? **The version that gets shit done!**

Okay, I get it if you have messy people in your house - if this is the case and they won't step up...you step up and claim a room/corner/table for you to be organised in. OR leave the house and focus on your shit away from the shit. E.g., a cafe or a park.

So a key to getting your shit done is to **get organised.**

Right - if you are sitting there going...*'My house is so messy. I can't get shit done or even read this book'* then put down the book right now and go and clean/tidy up. I am giving you permission now. Or put down the book and go and clean a drawer out. You will have a clear mind, I assure you.

But remember to come back to this book!

Hello?

Onto making a plan.

Get a diary and write that shit down. Work out what it is that you need to do.

Go back to chapter two if you need to - get clear on your goal/dream or clear on your action and put it in your diary or get a journal.

A note on journals - yes you can get fancy ones. And if that's your thang' then get them. But honestly, I am usually found writing in exercise books that are quickly thrown into my bag to carry around.

Don't *wait* till you have the perfect journal until you make a plan.

No excuses!

You may have heard of the SMART Goal Analogy. It's pretty good, but I add an E on the end, which not only sounds way cooler but is way more effective.

Side note: Setting goals in the way I am about to show you isn't for everyone. I get that. Some people are great with this, and to be honest, you should try it regardless, as you can learn some cool new shit! There are other great ways too - Vision Boards are fab also. I do use both this process and make a Vision Board. Google that if you think this would be helpful.

Remember this is just a guide and you will find that parts of this do blend into each other.

Check it out on the next bit and read on to do it yourself.

Specific - What specifically do you want to achieve?

What is the goal or dream? Remember to read chapter 2 on getting clear.

Get specific - rather than saying I want to lose weight. Could you use an amount? Or a dress size?

I want a new job, or I'll start a business. What area? What is your expertise? Do you need training - what kind of business?

I want to earn more money. How much? Specifically? Do you even know how much you need to live on? Ask yourself these questions plus more.

Measurable - Can this goal or dream be measured?

If it can't be measured, re-think it. How will you know that you are achieving it? You want to be able to measure the progress towards the goal.

Losing weight and getting fitter - is that losing half a kilo a week your measurement or running that flight of stairs at the beach within two weeks?

Earning more money - are you getting planned raises or if you are starting a business, are you tracking the profit?

Action - What are the steps or action you will need to take to achieve this goal?

Using the example of losing weight - what steps will you take? Do you need a hand with a Personal Trainer? Or locking out time in your diary to workout. Do you need to need to talk with your family to do this and get their support?

A new job, do you need to re-train at college? What are the steps around this? Will you need to move or travel further?

Earning more money - maybe a step could be talking to your boss or re-working your budget and losing Pay TV to save cash.

Realistic - How realistic is this goal?

Back to getting fitter...is it realistic to think that you can lose the weight that has taken years to accumulate to come off in weeks? No probably not. It may be more realistic to put together a twelve-month plan or add a time frame (see next step).

Changing jobs - wanting to be the CEO of your company when you are still in the mailroom is perhaps out of scope... unless this goal timeframe is longer? But let's not rule it out hey? But wanting to be a solicitor within six months isn't realistic. *On this step, get honest as well as realistic.*

~~Earning $100,000 when you are on $30,000 now isn't perhaps realistic if you haven't re-trained etc. yet... but again if the plan is longer and it's realistic…use it.~~

SCRAP THAT! In fact, don't listen to me, if your dream is to do that - do it! Your version of reality is probably different to mine anyway....who am I to say? Do your own thing while being realistic about the process. Remember the peeps who want to win the lottery but don't purchase a ticket?

Timely - By when do you want to achieve this goal?

Attach a time-frame to your goal or dream. It's interesting that when we give ourselves a date or time - we really do get shit done don't we?

Lose weight and get healthy by when? Three months? Six months? Twelve months? A birthday or special event perhaps.

Attach a date to when you will have that new job or business - rather than saying *'I'll get one next year...'* When next year? Attach a month or date and see what happens.

Same with the money thing - by when will have you achieved your goal. Even if it's five years out - it must have a date on it.

So there is your SMART goal strategy. There are some variations of this analogy everywhere...but I believe it's missing a **vital** part!

E - for EMOTION. See I told you it sounded better too...SMARTE! The E for emotion is the piece that joins the jigsaw of goal setting together. It really is, because it's your **why.**

Why are you setting this goal?

Now it's super easy to say *'Oh I want to fit into that suit or dress'* But really? Is that a great *why*?

Your *why* has to be so juicy it means that you will do anything to achieve it! So emotive that you will move mountains to get it done!

This part is so important I did a whole chapter on it. See chapter 3 for your *why*.

Make your plan/goal/dream. You have the steps so far.

What's stopping you?

Oh, that's right. **You.**

Okay, we will deal with you very soon.

Is this starting to make sense? All of these steps will begin to join together if you have persevered and pushed through this part of the book.

By the way, you can get started on actually making some SMARTE goals in a sec...keep going for now.

Lastly - a key component to making a plan is **accountability.**

Isn't it true that when we put it *out there* we will do something we feel obligated to follow through?

So tell somebody what you're going to do.

It could be your spouse or partner. It could be your children. It could be your work friends.

It could be a coach or a mentor. Telling someone that you're going to do something is an excellent way of pushing you to get your shit done. Accountability totally works. I know, I do it often.

If you need to...use social media! Put it on Facebook what you're going to achieve.

For example, you could use your health and say *'In six months I'm going to weigh 20 kilos less'.*

The fact that you've told people is a great deal of a push. *Wouldn't you agree?*

Someone I knew used accountability to the max a few years ago. He decided that he needed to stick to working out regularly (due to health reasons) So he devised a plan.

He disliked a particular radio personality (no names mentioned here) and told everyone he knew (yes everyone!) that he would write a cheque for $2000 to this person if he didn't fit in ten workouts in two weeks. Did he do it? You bet he did...the first week he did three workouts. The second week he started slow...but over the last three days he did seven! Yes, he spewed. And this story is a little extreme...but he didn't write that cheque.

You can get somebody who can keep track of you. Get a trainer or a coach who you can check in with every single week to make sure that this plan even comes to fruition.

Remember, it's linked to taking action - to doing something about it.

Actually, did you know that there's a Japanese term called 'Tsundoku' which means acquiring reading materials but letting them pile up in one's home without reading them. So, a lot of people will buy a book, for example: about getting their shit done and not read it because in their head they've already taken a step to rectify that issue. WTF?

Or they'll write down their plan, and knowing that they've written down their plan is enough for them to go *'Oh, well I've written it down now. It will come true.'*

No, this is where you get it wrong. It's actually about taking that action, reviewing the goal and the action and yes of course JFDI'ing.

Think about those people who have put plans and goals into place... they have taken action, and moved forward - therefore got their shit done.

What would happen if you didn't have a plan? It might not even happen, or it may not go to where you want it to be.

Let's back to those SMARTE goals again:

Specific

Measurable

Action

Realistic

Timely

Emotive

You should also be asking yourself some questions around this: What could you tweak or what could you adjust on that?

Is it realistic?
Is it timely?
Is it specific enough?
Do you get emotive around it?

For those of you who are having resistance about this and saying 'having a plan, that's not the way I work...' have a look at what you've done in the past.

What have you done in the past that didn't work?

> Insanity is doing the same thing over and over again, and expecting different results.
>
> Albert Einstein

It's not about having someone or something telling you what to, but discipline is the only way to go. By the way, discipline is not about punishment. It's about an activity that improves a skill in this instance.

I am one of those people that dislike like being told what to do.

Rules! No way! Viva la revolution and all that.

However, I know that being disciplined, having a plan, JFDIing, taking action...and all of those things will mean I get my shit done.

Sometimes you just got to bend your rules to suit what you need it to. If you're one of those people who like to have a checklist, go for it.

But...you are always going to have a to-do list. You do understand that? Don't you?

If you go, 'I don't know what to do, or what to start with...' do one of those things.

Write down all of the stuff that you need to do over the next few days.

Write it all down on paper and pick one item.

Then see how you feel afterward.

You may pick another item if you like.

A suggestion is to pick three items and see how you feel then. Are you are moving forward yet? Bit by bit, little by little...do something.

Even ticking off three items of your to-do list...is a lot better than sitting back and going *'I need to do A, B, C and all the rest...'*

Does that make sense?

Off you go then.

Make your plan.

Set your goals and get organised then keep going.

Why don't you share this chapter on social media with the following:

#SMARTEgoals

#discliplineisthenewblack

#7SecretsGetShitDone

I'll see you in the next chapter.

People don't plan to fail.

They fail to plan.

Name of goal/dream/plan: ....

Specific

What *specifically* do you want to achieve?

....
....
....
....
....

Measurable

Can this goal or dream be measured?

....
....
....
....
....

Action

What are the steps or action you will need to take to achieve this goal?

....
....
....
....
....

Realistic

How realistic is this goal?

....
....
....
....
....

Timely

By when do you want to achieve this goal?

....
....
....
....
....

Emotive

WHY are you setting this goal? Remember to make it juicy!

....
....
....
....
....

Chapter 7: Secret #7 Set a timer
AKA Chunk down your task into manageable bits

Now, this one is super easy.

If you're wondering how to get your shit done and you have opened it to this chapter, **set a timer!**

Use what you've got. You could use an oven timer. You could use your phone. You could use a stopwatch or clock. In fact, there are apps on your phone that will allow you to set timers.

Set a timer to get your shit done.

I work in a few ways. I sometimes use 25 minutes. Sometimes 50 minutes.

I sit down, do some writing...or do some blogging and after 25 minutes - I get up, have a stretch. Or I might have a cup of tea...or I might go for a quick walk, and then I come back for another 25 minutes.

This isn't new stuff either - go check out the *Pomodoro* Technique for more tips on the 25-minute thing.

You can use this for anything - housework, study or a workout. Giving yourself a time-frame to get something done means you push yourself to get it done.

Remember if you give yourself all day to get a task done, it takes all day or not at all!

On big projects, I'll often set a timer for 50 minutes.

When you've got a time frame attached to something, you know you will get shit done.

This works great with kids too. *'Tidy your room. Here's the timer, 10 minutes...and go!'*

So if your task needs to be done, chunk it down into the 25 minutes or 50 minutes, but not longer than 50 minutes because that's when you can get stiff or you can lose your concentration. I know you may be in 'flow.' But trust me, this shit works! Plus science backs me up - Google it!

Our brains get pretty distracted these days, and I'm going to blame the internet for that one.

If you want to read a book on how our brains are being rewired because of the internet - go and look up *'The Shallows' by Nicholas Carr*. He summarises that we have rewired our reading and learning techniques due to web browsing.

Think about it - when you read these days, you scan the pages and look for the pictures or hyperlink.

You read/scan constantly and getting into reading a proper book is hard to concentrate on. I know, it happens to me too. But I also know that I give myself a few minutes to stick to the book, knowing that my old reading habit is in my brain somewhere. *Doing both is possible.*

For the 25 or 50 min block of time - if you need to, turn your phone off and the notifications of email, etc. off too. There are also apps for your computer to prevent you from using the internet if you need help. There is indeed something for everything these days.

Go and do the work in your specified time and then come back after a 5-minute break.

If you need to put those chunks of time in your diary, do that too.

Whatever works for you. You can even use this technique at work, with your colleagues or team. You could also use it to gauge peoples productivity on a task. #toptip

Indeed, sitting down and typing is not my favourite thing to do on a long-term basis - but working for 25 minutes at a time...then having a stretch...putting a song and having a bit of a dance does work. How do you think this book was written? *Yep, in 25 min chunks.* True dat.

What are you waiting for? Grab that clock and go!

Why not use the following hashtags on social media to share what you are doing?

#25minsworksforme

#7SecretsGetShitDone

Oh my, we have reached secret number 7! But guess what? You get a bonus! Keep reading…

Bonus Chapter 8 Your beliefs.
AKA the shit you know.

Why do we focus on certain things?

Why do we do what we do?

Oh, huge questions here!

I'll give a quick example; there is a small car accident with a red and a white car. Five people witnessed the crash. *How many versions of the story are there?*

Probably seven, given there are two drivers. Some may say the white car crashed into the red car - others may say the opposite. What about the bike? What bike?

Why are there so many different stories happening?

It's because of your **focus.**

But also your **beliefs.**

You may or may not know this…but we can only focus on 5-7 things at any one time. Go look up Neuro Linguistic Programming (N.L.P) if you want to learn more about this concept.

The other stuff we either *delete, distort or generalise* based upon our beliefs.

Delete
Distort
Generalise

Have I lost you yet? I'll throw you an example to help;

Bob thinks he is unattractive. He has heard since a young age that he is not attractive. He has searched for evidence to confirm this (What he focus's on, he gets) and now believes this.

Carla thinks Bob is hot. She tells him so. Bob, however, will do one of three things with whatever Carla says about him. He will either *delete, distort or generalise* what she said to him - as he believes he is unattractive.

It goes a bit like this:

Carla says *"Bob, you are a hottie!"*

He says "_____" ignores it…. - he has deleted this information

He says *"What did you just say?"* or, *"You said I am hot? I'm not hot - the temperature is just fine"* - he has distorted this information

He says *"Oh, you must say that to everyone"* - he has generalised the information.

Get it?

So based upon this information - what are you not only focusing on now… but what are you deleting, distorting or generalising based upon what you believe?

What could you change?

Could you change your perception for a day and see what happens?

Who knows?

You might just change your life.

Food for thought

These chapters are for you to pick up and quickly read…then consider.

Enjoy.

Next minute

Sometimes I'm an impatient person. Are you?

I want to do things today/now/next minute.

Perhaps it's a part of me, or maybe it's part of our culture? We want things straight away; we want results now, we want to get things done yesterday. #amiright

We are rushing. We are 'nexting' all the time. Our brain even does it for us. We live a lot of our time in the…

…next minute.

See…you knew I would even say that. Your brain is doing it as you read this.

I am doing it as I type it.

We focus on what we are doing *next*.

We talk about what we are doing *next*.

We know what we are doing *next*.

I could go on.

There are books written about this stuff (Google away). Physiologically the average human brain does this (a bit of a caveman thing we still do) so much of the time, and sometimes we can't help it.

As humans, we naturally want to see things to the end. We naturally want to 'finish' things.

Yes, that explains why we (ok, me) will spend hours on Netflix watching four seasons of *Addictive drama* in a matter of weeks. It's the reason we want to *know* what happens at the end of the book, why we dislike spoilers of any sort.

Kinda funny really. Some may call it an addiction, but often we are just doing what our brain wants to do.

Not being able to finish things, get stuff done, etc. can lead us to frustration (there are probably more emotions I could add, but this chapter could get too long, hey?). I know I am guilty of cursing (who knew?) when the internet drops out, or when I get interrupted when I'm reading. I know of people who get physically violent when their computer game freezes. I am also sure you can reel off several occasions where something similar has happened too.

So, what is the answer?

Who knows the magic answer? I am pretty sure there are some scientists/researchers/cool peeps working on it though…For me - and perhaps for you - being aware that you are *nexting* or getting frustrated is the first step.

Recognising this and then taking a step back, viewing the situation from afar can perhaps alter what is happening. If it helps, imagine a friend looking at what you are doing and what would they say/do?

I'll give you an example if that helps:

So, a couple of years ago something happened to my internet at home. It was disconnected because someone had connected my neighbour but disconnected me in error. I had worked this out and was very cranky, to say the least.

Of course, I told my internet provider this, and their answer was to wait 14 days for someone to come out to have a *look*. Now, let's look at the big picture: I work from home, and my business relies on it. Without it means I can't work; therefore I can't connect with my clients, therefore can't make an income. In my head, it was the worst thing ever. Even worse than finding a nest of red-back spiders in my bbq (true story).

Anyhoo…I was super angry/cranky/cross/frustrated! You name it; I said it/did it. I was awful.

I was also *nexting* constantly.

What would happen if…? What will happen when…? What's going to happen to my business when…? The list was long and pretty sad. I was living in 'what if?' and all that happened was…that I lost the internet.

The solution to this?

My daughter (who was 11 at the time). She said to me *'Mum, why are you so angry about this? We should be happy with what we have. I know a lot of people in this world who don't have the internet...they don't even have food or money.'*

Wow.

Thanks, darling - I needed to hear that. She was right.

How very selfish of me to speak/act that way. It was only going to be 14 days, and here I was acting like a kid having a tantrum over a lollypop.

Instantly I was aware of what I was doing (the first step). Then her comment enabled me to view it from another angle.

This was all I needed to hear.

I changed my thoughts to gratitude for what we have. Thankful that I even have the opportunity to work from home in my own hours. Grateful that we have the technology to communicate around the world within seconds. Thankful that I can even afford the internet, let alone food.

What did I do for the next 14 days? I started calling people, connecting in person at networking meetings and handwriting notes/ cards to previous clients. Who would have known? The old fashioned way worked, and my business not only survived but thrived as a result! All thanks to my darling child who's simple words prevented me from two weeks of un-resourceful anger and frustration.

Living in frustration, anger or a simmering irritation is detrimental to your mental state. I'd call on some stats to prove it, but I can't be arsed as I know you already know this - don't you?

As for living in the present - it is incredibly calming.

Meditation helps with this, focusing on one task is similar too. Ever lost yourself in creating something and felt better afterward? It's meant to feel good.

Feeling moments of anxiousness, fear or unease only feeds that voice in your head. *You know the one*...it's currently telling me that no-one will read this book and that I am wasting my time.

I'll never forget reading something recently about people with brain injuries in the frontal cortex (the front bit). This is the part of the brain where we think about the future. They studied these people, and they were incredibly calm. No sign of anxiousness. They were not worried about the future - as their brain didn't know there was even a 'future' to be worried about.

How about that? Take from that small story what you will.

I know I will continue being aware of when I am living in 'what if..?'.

And I hope you will too.

Why do we leave things to the last minute?

What is with that?

I have been procrastinating over this chapter - telling myself that I will get it done by noon. It's now 11.45am, and I have less than 30 mins battery on my laptop.

Do I love the 'pressure' of a deadline? *Is it the rush? Perhaps....?*

Given that my version of living on the edge is two coffees a day and listening to Metallica on occasion. Okay, so maybe it is the rush…?

Seriously though, **why do we leave things till the last moment?**

Cramming for exams the night before, getting up early to get a deadline done or putting that bid in on eBay four seconds before it ends? *Or is that just me?*

Oh, I can justify the entire thing! *'I work better under pressure.'*

'I do my best with an imminent deadline' blah blah - I am sure you can use some of these excuses yourself.

Of course, what I am talking about is that big word 'procrastination.' Yep, we have all been there! It's estimated that over 70% of academic students leave things to the last minute. Makes sense really.

Gosh, I can even vouch to being the best procrastinator of all time - it took me 20 years to get around to applying for my Australian Citizenship.

Why is that? Because it wasn't really an essential thing to do. I had no time frame on HAVING to get it done. Even though I really wanted to get it - having no timeframe attached to this initially, meant that I didn't have to do it.

Which brings me to **you**, my friend.

What are you not doing because there is no timeframe attached to it?

What are you procrastinating about because you 'don't' have to do it?

What are you not doing now, that you could be doing today to move you forward in your life/career/relationship/business/responsibilities*

*delete as appropriate.

What could you achieve if you sucked it up and JFDI'd it? Yes, you know what that stands for.

What is stopping you? I'll give you a hint…it's probably **you**.

Where has being a self-proclaimed procrastinator gotten me? In some areas, not very far - I'll be honest.

Now I am not being hard on myself (or you) but recognising a trait that doesn't work is a good idea - because you can change this. It just takes a bit of discipline and self-evaluation.

When you set a goal - set a timeframe with it.

When you say you are going to do something - get accountable by telling someone.

Then the key to taking ACTION…

…is taking fucking ACTION!

There is no secret. Oh, apart from one thing.

You need to have a good reason WHY you are doing that thing.

WHY? WHY? WHY?

WHY are you doing it?

It needs to be juicy!

It needs to be emotive.

It needs to drive you.

If it doesn't stir you up, it's not juicy enough.

Simple.

That weight you want to lose. The reason you want to lose it cannot be 'I want to fit into that dress/suit.'

Make the goal so emotive NOTHING WILL STOP YOU!
Procrastination?
Pfft!

Whatever.

I'll repeat for the dummies.

Set the goal.

Attach a date (or timeframe)

Get accountable

Is your WHY juicy enough?

Take ACTION!

So, me? Yep, I still procrastinate in some areas of my life - hey! I'm not perfect...who is? Aiming for perfection is a shitty standard, and I'll probably write another book on that another day.

But to give you an idea of why I am writing? Because eventually I can add these chapters up and finish the book you are reading. And yes, I do have a timeframe, I am accountable (to you guys now!), my WHY is very very juicy and writing this is taking action.

See it works!

What will you do now?

JFDI peeps.

Care Less

I care less these days.

It's nice.

But first, let me explain...

Gosh, life is tricky. All those people, all those different opinions/attitudes/personalities. Not to mention differing values and intentions.

We sometimes think we know what people are thinking. We think we know what they are going to do or say.

Why is that?

Because we compare.

We compare to us.

What *we* would do or say.

How *we* would react. I believe we are so inside our heads and that we don't *think* enough.

We are so inside our heads we think people are talking about us, thinking about us and writing about us.

Think about this (get it?) - when you see a post on Facebook about someone...who know the type of post I am talking about...directed at 'someone.' They may not have mentioned a name. But sometimes for a split second, you think it's about *you*.

That's how much inside our heads we are! *Kinda crazy hey?*

Even if you don't do it regularly, you can remember a time when you have. *Can't you?*

That's how big our ego is. It even talks to us through other peoples actions.

But what if you asked yourself a different question?

What if you asked *'What does it mean to them?'*

'What are they going through that means they are reacting that way?'

What if this meant that you no longer judged?

What if?

Is it a waste of energy to think about what others are saying/doing?

How else could you use that energy?

Have you ever wondered why someone was so interested in what you were doing or up to? They were so involved with you and *why* you were doing something?

Well, it's easy to think about someone else. It's easy to think/blame/point the finger/criticise/put down someone else - focusing on themselves is harder.

Get it?

They go for the easy option.

I had a conversation (ok it was more than a convo) with someone a while back. They said how I was a terrible mother, never spent time with my kid, never spent money on her and overall was a shitty parent. Wow- thanks for that. #not

Luckily I knew at a deep level that I was none of these things - and instantly recognised this as a reflection of them. They were all of those things, yet pointed the finger at me. Did I fight back? Yes, I admit - I said a few harsh words to that person, but I didn't really fight as I knew it was incorrect. I felt sorry for them and walked away.

What would have happened if I hadn't worked on myself? Hadn't spent a few years learning about ME and why/how I do stuff? Perhaps a different story?

I was glad it happened as it further concreted into my mind how far I had come.

I want to say that I don't judge people 100%, but it's probably nowhere near that figure, as the subconscious runs deeper than you think...therefore you judge without knowing that you are.

However, I feel lighter at not judging.

I feel lighter in my decision making.

I enjoy people a lot more.

I move through life with a lot more ease, knowing that I care less about people think/say about me.

It's a nice feeling.

I smile more.

I love more.

I give more.

I am more.

So what or who are you focusing on today?

I failed

I am a failure.

I have failed to so many times, and it is absolutely ridiculous.

I fail every single day.

I fail every single week.

I fail every single month.

And yes, I fail every single year.

Does it make me feel good? Not all the time. But, it's not that bad.

In fact, the more I fail, the more I succeed...is that odd?

So why does failing mean that I succeed?

Because it's FEEDBACK.

Every single time I fail...I learn something new.

Every single time I mess up, there is always a lesson.

It is all feedback.

Wouldn't you agree?

Would you agree my friend, that every time you have made a mistake...you have learnt a lesson?

Whether you have regrets or not...this isn't about living in regret. It's about what you have learnt and can change for the future. *Can you see that?*

There is a gift in every situation. Believe me; there have been some doozies! At the time you think *'No good can come of this.'*

But oh!...there is always a gift!

Some people will make mistakes...time and time again.

You know the people, the ones who choose the wrong partner or wrong job all the time.

The ones who seem to be in a pattern and repeat that pattern day in day out. Hang on...that sounds like me! Or you!

Look, we're human. And as humans, we like to do things in patterns.

You know the type of thing...you brush your teeth the same way every day. You drive the same way to work every single day.

See, we like patterns.

So it wouldn't surprise you to understand, that you even make patterns in *failing*.

Have you ever find yourself thinking *'Why have I done that exact same thing again?'*

Then you kick yourself not remembering.

You really can't help yourself; it's in your nature.

So what's the solution? Well, they do say the definition of insanity is to do the same thing over and over and expect a different outcome.

Apparently, Einstein said this. What a clever dude.

So - back to the solution - don't do the same thing over and over again.

Just recognise what you are doing and either stop it, tweak it, or try something else. You may need to tweak it a lot…you may need to tweak it a little bit…you may need to try something totally different.

And that's okay. It's all feedback.

Just try again.

Then try again, until it works.

Sometimes just having the 'awareness' that you are creating a pattern that doesn't help you, can do the trick.

Slight side note: There is something that I ask my child at least twice a week when I pick her up from school…I ask her:

'What did you fail at today?'

Her answers are pretty cool! I hear about the lessons that she has learnt, and how she can improve on that the next time.

Lastly, I'll share with you something that I do whenever I'm about to try something new.

I go into a project/situation (or whatever it is) with the notion that I will fuck it up.

You heard me.

I go into it with the opposite mindset of *'I hope I don't fail this'* or *'I hope nobody notices that I mess up.'*

Sometimes I plan to fuck it up!

Knowing that I will always learn a great lesson by doing so. And guess what? I don't always fuck it up.

By doing this, I take the pressure off myself...to enjoy the journey and learn something new.

After all, we can't all be perfect can we?

So my friend, what are you going to fuck up today?

Ask for help

What are you doing?

Why are you still faffing around? Why are you still procrastinating about the little things? Why haven't you put yourself first?

You're asking yourself - *What is wrong with me?*

Honestly, my friend, that question is a loaded one.

Asking yourself *'What is wrong with me?'* can lead you down a dark, dark hole.

Honestly, I think it's one of our ego's most favourite questions. All those voices inside of your head going around and around and around.

Day in, day out.

Week in, week out.

And yes, years and years and years too...

You do realise, that I'm writing to me.

Except, that I'm writing *you* instead of *me*.

Because we're all the same aren't we?

We're all imperfectly perfect human beings.

While we all have a unique personality, we are all essentially the same.

I've coached many, many people over the last few years, and quite honestly we do the same patterns. I could probably count on one hand the patterns that we'll have, and we all share this across the world.

We may do them all differently - but I find it fascinating...*that we think nobody else feels the same way!*

We're in our head so much that we think that no-one else can feel what we feel.

That is utter bullshit.

The biggest problem we have is pretending that we don't have any problems! We all have bloody problems!

If only we shared more often, then I believe...That we would connect more.

We would sympathise more.

We would be more patient.

We would empathise more.

We would be kinder to ourselves.

Isn't that the point?

To be kinder to ourselves?

We hold our standards so high...to nearly impossible standards.

So for some people, they don't even try.

Then we pass that shit onto our children. We pass so much onto our kids; we have no idea what the consequences can be - as they are growing up into adulthood. It's true...our children, or the people around us all role-model what they hear, see and feel.

Look at your parents, for example. Or whoever bought you up. What have you mimicked? What are you subconsciously followed? What are you doing today, that you said you would never do?

It's not too late my friend. Being aware of your patterns, being aware of what you say and of course being aware of what you do. *Is always the first step.*

It's totally okay, to admit that you have problems. Don't be stubborn for goodness sake! Do you think you can shoulder all that crap all on your own?

Ask for help.

Tell a friend.

If need be, get professional help.

It's okay to be vulnerable. It's okay to tell the world that things are not going awesomely.

Yes, yes....you don't want people feeling sorry for you, do you?

Guess what? I think you'll find that they just want to help.

Sometimes being an adult does suck. Sometimes, no one is there to pat our backs when we achieve something cool...so why don't you pat your own back? Celebrate the wins! Goddamnit…celebrate the losses too - while you're at it.

Tell the whole world how awesome you are! Tell the entire world what you achieved in the last 12 months.

Or...tell me. I'll pat your back for you :)

I repeat for the dummies:

Ask for help.

It's okay to be vulnerable.

Celebrate the wins.

Celebrate the losses.

And know that you are human.

Nuff said.

Near miss

So before I sat down to write this, a car pulled out in front of me. My split-second reaction on the brakes meant that I missed that car by about .5cm.

Am I happy that my brakes work? Hell yes! Am I happy that I am ok?

Shit yes.

That was probably the closest I have ever become to being in a crash with another car.

PHEW! Thank you, Universe too.

Anyway, enough about my dramas…But it got me thinking about other 'near misses' I have had in life.

I am not just talking physical misses, although there must have been a few.

I am talking about life decisions that turned out for the best and that perhaps…I dodged a bullet.

I have many a story, as I am sure you do too. From walking away from toxic relationships to taking a bus instead of walking and missing a gas explosion that killed a couple of people in Ireland (That was a gut feeling that my friends and I shouldn't walk that day.)

Was it a conscious decision? Or a *gut* feeling?

You know what I am talking about...that feeling...that something is a bit 'off.' That feeling when you walk into a room where you can cut the tension with a knife. *You get me.*

Science is now proving that our gut and heart feelings are *real*. There are brain cells in those areas that make us physically feel something. Being broken-hearted is now a *real* thing. Go Google the 'Heart study' if you have time.

So working with a conscious decision (me slamming on the brakes) to being in touch with our gut - what choices are you making or more importantly ignoring?

Are you doing things that you know that don't *feel right*? It could be putting someone else needs before another.

It could be agreeing to do something...even though you don't want to.

It could be not doing something because you could hurt a persons feelings.

It could be that feeling you get when you walk into work.

It could be that feeling you get when you walk into your home.

It could be anything.

We live busy lives - we are running and running on that treadmill of life...and we can forget to check-in with ourselves. We forget that our bodies know best. We know instinctively our gut/heart feelings are right.

Why are you not trusting yourself?

What will it take to trust yourself?

What do you need to remember, to trust yourself?

Do you, in fact, trust at all?

And if you don't, or you can't - then it's time for the basics.

Are you eating well? Are you drinking enough water? Are you getting enough sleep? Are you moving daily? Listen to that self-talk....what is it saying?

If your basics list is low, make it a priority. STAT.

If not, then maybe the next time a car pulls out in front of you- you may not see it.

Being scared

I get scared, quite a lot. Not of course by ghosts or ghouls...but by putting myself *out there*.

In fact, and being scared by ghosts on a regular occasion would be far better than the feelings I get almost daily.

Being scared by a ghostly apparition would be easy! At least I have a rough idea of what it looks like. At least I have a good idea of what it sounds like. At least I have a rough idea of what it would do to me.

But being scared by 'putting myself out there,' is a different type of scary, hey?

Any fear that I have seen felt or heard over the years starts chipping away at me. Memories of being taunted at school, memories that overcome my senses...memories of speaking up.

Isn't it funny, when you start thinking about your past...more stuff pops up. Memories that you that you've put away for many years starts coming back to you.

I've just remembered a teacher at primary school, who for some reason took a dislike to me for no reason. (honestly, I was a good kid).

The only thing I can remember about that year at school (I think I was about eight years old) was that I sat outside the classroom a lot. She spoke to me terribly, and it's probably why I still don't know my times- tables at this age. It's all good though, I have done a lot of forgiveness work, and she is now on my list. Mrs. Paige - if you are reading this. You might want to work through some of your stuff!

So back to being scared about putting myself *out there*. It's a fear that we all have - I am sure you have it too. If you don't, well done. :)

I know a lot of it is about giving less of a shit about what people think.

And as time goes on, I really do care less about that. I can't wait till I am 90 years old - imagine what I will say! Haha!

Fears - they say we all have two main fears.

Fear of not being good enough.
Fear of not being loved.

These two concerns are involved in every decision we make. Go back to any decision you have made this week, and you will find they link back to both of these.

It's pretty interesting hey?

In fact, they say our brain is wired to fear more than to succeed. Think back to cave-man times if you will...listening out for the sabre-toothed tiger while we slept.

So a question I have been asking myself recently is:

What would you do if you weren't scared?

This opens up a realm of ideas, doesn't it?

Can you imagine?

Well, that's exactly what I want you to do.

Imagine.

So, what would you do?

Why are you here?

Why are you here? Why are you even on this planet?

Have you ever asked yourself this?

Perhaps you have pondered it as a child, or daydreamed about it as an adult.

BTW it's totes ok if you haven't even considered it too.

Do I have the answer? Probably not, but hey, it's fun to think about isn't it?

I do know why I am **not** here for though.

I am not on this planet to whinge, whine, complain or bicker. I am not on this planet to criticise me or others.

I am not on this planet to lie to myself or others.

I am not on this planet to ridicule or demean.

I am not on this planet to count the hours, days till whenever.

I am not on this planet to just survive.

Make a list, why don't you?

When you make a list of why you are **not** here - it's easier to think about why you **are** here.

Work backward if that helps.

I am here on this planet to live.

I am here on this planet to dig deeper.

I am here on this planet to care less about conforming to days/times/ weeks. I live it to my schedule.

I am here on this planet to empathise.

I am here on this planet, to tell the truth.

I am here on this planet to encourage.

I am here on this planet to take responsibility.

Copy my list for inspiration if you need to.

What am I doing with this knowledge?

Changing peoples lives, one at a time.

Starting with you.

You are what you say you are

Remember hearing that as a kid? You probably said it too.

It's true.

You are what you say you are.

I am fat.
I am poor.
I am a whinger.

Say that enough...and guess what? You will be fat, poor and a whinger to boot!

Saying shit like that day in, day out - is effectively self hypnotising yourself.

You say something enough...you believe it. You hear something enough...you start to *believe* it.

Us humans have a need to be right. So our fabulous brains will help us get to what we are saying.

Continually saying that you are fat, will only hard-wire that bullshit into your brain...and it will act accordingly.

Another point....gossiping about others, saying nasty things about people and generally pointing out peoples odd-bits is actually all *you*.

You wouldn't point them out if you didn't see it somewhere in yourself. Think about it. *I dare you.*

Back to those conversations you wish you never had. *'Oh look at her arse'*.... even if inside your head. What's going on with your arse?

You wouldn't even say/think it...if you didn't have an issue with yours.

It's not too late to turn that crap around.

Never too late.

I am beautiful.
I am wealthy.
I keep my mouth shut and encourage.

Do you know that age-old saying *'If you have nothing good to say, then don't say anything at all'* bizzo? Absolutely spot on Gran!

It may take practice, and that's ok. It may take years, and that's ok too. At least you are giving it a go.

So what are you going to say today, my friend?

Too comfortable with pain

Dictionary:

familiar

1. well known from long or close association.

~

Your pain. It's familiar.

Pain is familiar.

It is.

Think about it. Staying in a job you hate, staying in a marriage that is just a shell, paying the minimum rate on that credit card, feeling the tightness around your waist in your favourite pair of jeans.

It's all familiar.

So familiar in fact, that that you feel comfortable in that pain.

So comfortable - that stepping out of that situation is more painful to think about – than to actually do.

'I'm trying'...I hear you say. Are you trying? Are you actually trying?

Or giving a half-arsed go?

You are so comfortable in that job. That job that gives you that dull ache in your chest as Sunday night comes around. You are now comfortable with that ache. You are now comfortable with knowing that your talents and skills are being wasted, day by day, week by week, year by year. You are comfortable with that pain. *It's familiar.*

You are so comfortable in that marriage. That marriage that feels empty and without love. You are now comfortable with that feeling. You are now comfortable with lack of communication, fun, and laughter in a partnership. You are comfortable with that pain. *It's familiar.*

You are so comfortable with paying off that debt at the minimum rate. That debt that gives you the dreads every time the statement comes in the mail. You are now comfortable with living at this level, this level that gives you no joy or fun. You are comfortable with that pain. *It's familiar.*

You are so comfortable with the extra weight. That weight that stops you from going swimming with your loved ones or prevents you from letting go. You are now comfortable with living with the feeling of heaviness, creaky knees, breathlessness and being uncomfortable. You are comfortable with that pain. *It's familiar.*

Need I go on?

*'But I am *insert excuse here*…How can I change this?'*

It's up to you. But I'd suggest you start with **you.**

That's it.

Start at the source.

I can give you lists, strategies, ideas and more. But really my friend, it's down to **you**.

Raise your confidence, self-esteem, self-love, and appreciation. *'But that's too easy! Surely that isn't the answer'.*

Okay then.

Don't do that.

Do something else, follow another trend, read another article on the newest magical pill from the Amazon.

Or not.

Start by loving you.

Do things that you love to do.

Do things that make you laugh.

Do things that fill you with joy.

Oh, my friend, you may have forgotten. But with a little thought, you can remember.

That song you used to listen to and shake your body to.

That moment of joy from connecting with a friend and sharing.

That feeling you got when you moved daily.

That thing you created.

That thing you taught somebody else.

That's right...you can remember.

Do this.

Love you first.

Then when you feel like you are making progress, make that list. Get that strategy. Do that course.

Just don't get familiar with that feeling that you will do it tomorrow. Or on Monday. Or January. Or when the kids are at school. Or after that important task needs to be done for work. Or when you have time.

You don't have any of this.

You have now. Today. This minute. Now go.

Plan A or B?

Inspired by desperation.

Ever heard those words?

Ever get inspired to do something when you are desperate?

Ever been jolted into *action* by desperate times?

Isn't it interesting that we do this kind of stuff?

I suppose the reason I am thinking about this, is I have been noticing people making changes in their lives only when it gets 'desperate.'

When the doctor tells you that you have pre-diabetes and you need to change your diet.

When the surgeon tells you that knee replacements are imminent.

When you get to the last dollar in your bank account.

When the company you work for starts making job cuts.

I won't go on, as I don't want to make this a depressive chapter today.

But I think you get me.

Why does it have to get to the desperate point? Or does it have to get to an extreme point to make the change?

What is the answer? What do you do?

I know that when I have been guilty of doing this many many times. I also know that sometimes the best in me comes out when I am pushed.

I produce my best work when *I have no option* left.

Weird huh?

A friend of mine Brad Burton (Motivational Speaker/Business owner/ Founder of 4Networking in the UK) says that if you have a plan B in business. You won't stick to your plan A. That makes sense, doesn't it?

You could apply this to any area of your life. Having a plan B = you may not believe in plan A.

Food for thought for sure.

I have no answer for this.

Perhaps there is no answer?

Opportunity or obligation

Getting up early. Sucky? Or awesomeness?

If you know me at all, I am an early-bird...and guess what? I even catch that worm. In fact, it's 4.35am as I write this.

So getting up early is an *opportunity* for me.

It's an opportunity to get my work done and out; it's an opportunity to do what I need to do before being interrupted by a child/the world/ the phone/other people.

It's also an opportunity that I love.

Obligation. So let's use getting up early as the example here - is it an obligation for you? Do you feel obliged to do it? What is the feeling attached to that?

There's quite a difference between the two, hey?

The word *obligation* even feels blah. *Opportunity* nearly has a tinkly sound to it (when I say it in my head.)

Totes different I reckon.

What a great question to ask yourself today!

Is this an opportunity? Or an obligation?

Changing your health is an opportunity, not an obligation. Is it not? An opportunity to live longer, through life and move with ease.

If you view changing your health as an obligation, see the dictionary meanings below....Then you won't like it. How could you change that view?

Well, I know that I dislike people telling me what to do...and I think there are a few of you who will agree with me on that one. So being told that I have to look after my health...isn't going to push me any further.

In fact - it would stall me. *Does that sound familiar?*

You make your own rules.

When you listen to others - especially the media…You would be surprised by how much that affects us; it can mean that we start to feel obligated to 'join' in.

It's another weird cave-man thing. Being part of a tribe etc. etc. Luckily we have moved past foraging for food naked...or have we? #joke

Turn whatever it is that you want to do - whether it be your health, career, finances, relationships into an opportunity.

An opportunity to improve or change something.
An opportunity to change someone's life (even your own).
An opportunity to create a new path.

An opportunity to create a new role model for others to follow. An opportunity to take control of an area of your life. An opportunity to change careers or re-train.
An opportunity to see how far you can make it.

Start using the word opportunity more often in your day-to-day language and see what changes.

A real-life example for me about a year ago was that something awful happened (a personal thing) and instead of sitting in victim mode - I turned it into an opportunity. Instantly flipping those thoughts changed *everything*. Now I am even thankful for that circumstance. Call me crazy...but this shit works!

So what is it today for you, my friend? An opportunity?...or an obligation?

dictionary.com

opportunity

a time or set of circumstances that makes it possible to do something.

obligation

an act or course of action to which a person is morally or legally bound; a duty or commitment.

Without judgement

You judge.

I judge.

We all judge others.

Can you go for one day without doing it?

I can hear some of you saying *'I don't judge others.'*

Do you really? Is it even possible not to?

Your beliefs from a very young age and onwards are what makes us 'us.' Our subconscious is so in charge...and we think we are the ones in control!

Guess again, peeps!

You are totally not in control of your thoughts and actions.

Things we have heard, seen and felt are all in that amazing brain of yours. Things like the TV shows you watched as a kid (even in the background), stuff your parents or your family said, your teacher's opinions - the list goes on.

Your opinions are not even your own. They are someone else's.

Who's, are they? Who influenced you? I am 100% sure that you can't list them all as you are not consciously aware of it.

And that's ok. Us humans can't help it.

So do you judge? Do you judge other peoples actions, words, thoughts or purpose?

What are you comparing it to?

You.

What *you* would do if.... What *you* would say if... What *you* would feel if... How *you* would react if... How *you* would cope if…?

Guess what? It's not even about you.

You have no clue as to what is going on in peoples heads (nor do you want to!).

We are all so uniquely different - even identical twins are different. They have different personalities, even though they grow up in the same household and effectively see the same kind of stuff as they grow up.

There has been a heap of 'twin studies' over the years - one of them I remember was about a set of boy twins who grew up with an alcoholic father and drug addict mother. One of the boys grew up to be a drug addict. The other grew up to be a lawyer.

They were both asked the same question of how they became who they are today. They both answered *'What else could I be?'*

Interesting hey?

So back to the point.

You don't know what people are thinking. You do know what you are thinking though - and that's the bit you can control.

Having an awareness about other peoples beliefs will make you a nicer person to deal with. It's not even like you need to ask questions about them - just know they are not like you.

So what they say/do/feel/ask/see is based upon their stuff.

Not yours.

Try not to judge people for just a few days and see what happens to your world. It's not an easy task - but certainly a do-able one.

See if your opinions alter, see if your communication with others are easier and see if you put less pressure on *you*.

Do you save the best for last?

Gosh, this one shits me. Saving stuff 'for best.'

I even do it myself sometimes! I have some amazing smelly candles, and I caught myself 'saving' them for God knows when the other day…Yes, that's right, saving a smelly candle for the 'best' time to make them smell. WTF? *I am laughing as I type this, as it's quite ridiculous!*

I know people (not naming names) that will 'save' their perfume for best. Or their new sexy undies…or shoes! Oh dear God - it's crazy!

When is best?

Is it best for your funeral? Yes, you will smell great at that point, so perhaps you will need it then.

I knew people back in the UK who had plastic on their lounge, clearly saving the feel of the fabric on their bums for 'best.' Then there is the best china, crystal wine glasses, best coat or even whole room! I am sure you can add more to that list.

What are you waiting for? When is best? What are you saving for best or later?

Say yes

What if you said *yes*, more?

Now let me be clear; I am not referring to adding more to your responsibilities as a parent/worker, etc.

I am talking about saying *yes* to opportunities.

I heard on the radio just this week of a young man that decided to do a *new* thing every week for twelve months. He would do a dance class one week, try new food and say *yes* to opportunities that came as a result of him doing new things.

Doing more = seeing/hearing more.

It was inspirational to hear him talking about this experience. He said he had had the best year of his life so far! How cool is that?

Another example: I was talking to some friends recently about my plans for Christmas Day (feeding homeless through my local charity NeedaFeed), and my friend yelled out *'Yes! I'll do it too!'*. I didn't even ask her to join us. She told me that she had recently started saying *yes* to things and she was thoroughly enjoying her experiences.

Pretty cool huh?

What benefits do people get from doing this? Gosh, where do I start?

Feeling good about themselves...feeling good about helping/doing things with others...learning more about others (and themselves)... growing...increasing self-confidence...increasing self-esteem...you get the idea.

Someone wise once told me that if I was feeling bad about myself, I should help another. It's stuck with me for a while now and when I feel low...I help someone.

Interestingly, when you think about others, your brain doesn't have time to think about you. Try it! *Or, can you remember a time when you did this?*

So back to saying *yes*.

You could include saying *yes* to yourself for this year and onwards. Making time out for you.

Scheduling in time for moving and eating well. Saying *yes* to learning about your body and your mindset...you know that when you do that...you do in-turn, help others/kids/friends/partners.

What could you achieve by saying *yes* to you?

Great topic, I think you would agree.

So, what will you be saying *yes* to?

Watching or taking part

Some important questions to ponder:

Are you watching life pass you by? Or are you taking part?

Are you letting life 'happen' to/for you? Or are you in control?

Are you listening to the rain and letting it soothe your soul? Or are you whining that your hair will get ruined?

What are you doing?

Green and growing or ripe and rotting

Are you green and growing? Or ripe and rotting? What an odd thing to think about.

I heard this term a few years ago, and it really resonated with me. I've heard it from several people since and it still gets me thinking.

Imagine you are an apple.

What kind of apple are you? Are you learning new things, creating new experiences, meeting new people? Are you a growing apple?

Or are you ripe? But inside you are rotting and sitting in the same ol' situation, same job, same friends or same health.

What kind of apple do you actually want to be?

How could you grow?

What could you change?

Do you even want to change or make a difference?

And by the way, it's ok if you don't want to learn and grow. There is no right or wrong.

But if this topic is stirring you up - and this could be anything from sadness to anger...perhaps you are ready to make a change.

Otherwise, it would cause zero emotion. Kinda funny hey?

So tell me, my friend, what kind of apple are you?

What walks in the mother, runs in the child

Gosh, this statement ran chills down my back several years ago when I first heard it.

Really? How could such a short sentence change everything I have done/said/thought/been?

Yep. It sure did.

Think about it. This isn't just for the mothers out there either… it's for the fathers too.

What are your children doing?

How are they acting?

What do they do that bothers you?

Flip it back to you.

Are you doing the same or similar? Or is your partner?

NOTE: Don't play the blame game here. Look at yourself with honesty and really consider if you are the reason they do their shit.

It's not them. It's not their fault. It's probably you. Hey, it's ok. At least you have noticed it.

At least you are aware of it.

Now you can change this.

What can you do? Learn patience, be helpful, talk nicely to others, be compassionate, encourage others, smile, laugh and love.

Be all of those things and more. See what happens in your offspring.

Have faith that they will follow in your footsteps.

But only YOU can take the first step.

So what will you do today?

Forgive

I forgive you.

Those were the first words that started me on this journey of self- improvement.

Blaming others for my situation was not working. In fact, it was sending me backward.

Being the blamer was a role I had fit into very well. It's easy, isn't it? To point the finger? It's so easy to think/say/feel/see/hear that someone else is responsible for your problems. It's so easy because it probably comes naturally as people around us do it too. Or is that just me?

So *forgiveness* was the first step.

Do I forgive them? Do I forgive him? Do I forgive her? Do I forgive?

No.

I forgive me.

I forgive myself, and I let go of blame.

I took responsibility for my actions/thoughts and let go of the past.

After all, all that shit had made me who I am today. I am even quite thankful for what happened.

Kinda odd, but true.

By the way - this was not about condoning what they did. It was about me.

What a relief to do this!

What a weight off of my shoulders (it even felt like I was walking lighter). The emotion I was carrying around, the blame I was carrying around was heavy...and tiring.

God, I was tired.

Not so now.

I forgive me.

I forgive myself.

I love myself.

It's okay; you can let go now.

What are you focusing on?

The power of *focus* is a strong one.

Ever buy a new car, and suddenly everyone has that car?

Ever been pregnant (or your partner) and suddenly all you see is pregnant ladies?

I could go on - but you are intelligent enough to understand that this happens all the time.

It's your focus. Your focus is now focusing on that car/woman/whatever - they were always there.

Weren't they?

They were my friend. It was you that changed, not the people around you.

Do you know how many things are going on right now around and to you? Think about it....count them. How many? I bet you $1000 that you can't count them.

That's it...you can hear things can't you (when you focus). You are breathing.

You can feel the chair underneath your bum now I have mentioned it....your little toe in your shoe now I have mentioned it.

What else? Can you smell anything? Taste anything?

I am sure you are reading this and processing the words too...how many things?

It's a tad crazy...but there are about 1.2 million things going on right now around you.

Don't try to count as I am sure your brain will explode! *God knows who counted them in the first place...*

Anyhoo...so us humans can actually only process about 5-7 things at any one time. Think about that for a sec. By the way, I am not entering into an argument about men and multitasking either...

5-7 things! And that's a good day! What about the days you are highly emotional? Happy or sad?

Ever driven home from somewhere and got there thinking 'I don't remember that drive, did I run a red light?' I'll bet that you were thinking about something pretty important (or not?) and your brain went into auto-control and capped out.

It will do that (a bit like saving itself from blowing up).

Gosh, don't you love the brain?

There are reasons you will focus on one thing or another, and I'll save that for another day, but my point is that you will get what you focus on!

An example if this help:

...and yes this applies to any area of your life.

Are you finding that you are attracting the same kind of man or woman into your life? Saying I don't want to attract anyone older than me? Shorter than me? Whatever that 'thing' is... then you find that they are popping up everywhere?

IT'S BECAUSE YOU ARE FOCUSING ON THAT THING!

Another example to help you out:

I don't want to be fat, in pain, uncomfortable blah blah.

YOU WILL GET THIS - AS YOU ARE FOCUSING ON IT.

So an easy fix is to be clear on what you do want. It's super easy to say what you don't want, isn't it?

But do you know what you do want?

Get clear on that and see where your focus takes you.

Off you go.

Care even less

Bigger than normal language warning here

So, do you give a fuck?

Do you care what people think of you?

Of your career, your love life, your health or your home/where you live?

Really. Do you?

I know you may say that you don't give one...but at a deeper level do you?

What are you doing to 'fit in'?

What are you still doing to make sure you keep the friends you have had for years? Yes even the ones who annoy the shit out of you.

Why aren't you the real 'you?'

What is stopping you from giving less of a fuck?

I know. And you know why too.

You know why you are playing small and fitting in.

You know why you don't 'say something' to rock the boat/ make a difference/have an opinion *insert your version here.

You know why you don't tell people your achievements/dreams/ideas.

You know why you don't speak up.

You are scared.

A friend will tell you it's OK.

A parent will tell you that it's OK too.

But I won't.

And it's not OK. No way. Not on my watch. Stop being scared.

Stop playing small.

Stop fucking around with your life and your dreams.

You do care what people think - otherwise, you would stick your neck out.

You do care what others think of you - otherwise, you would change your career.

You do care what your partner thinks - otherwise, you would change that thing/speak up/move out.

You do care what your friends and family think - otherwise you would offend them by saying no.

What if?

What if you didn't give a fuck? And you know I am not referring to the not giving a fuck irresponsible/teenage mentality here.

What if you weren't afraid and actually didn't give a fuck about what people thought about you?

What if you stood out?

What if...by not giving a fuck - you propelled your life forward and without regret?

What fucking if?

Stop trying to fit in and play small. Let go and let this year be the year of not giving a fuck.

I wonder how far it will take you?

Jumping or dipping your toe in?

Are you one of those people that dip their toe into the water before they get in a pool or one of those people who inch...inch by inch...into the water because they're scared of that fresh water feeling?

Or are you someone who dives right in or, in fact...does a bomb?

I was down at the beach this morning, and I was watching people getting into the pool after my swim.

I was contemplating on these people getting in very, very carefully. *I'm wondering, perhaps...if that's how they approach life?*

It's just a question to you my friend, so think about it.

What do you do when you get into the ocean or a pool? Are you jumping in?

Because you know what? I did a massive bomb, and even the ladies there laughed at me saying, *'We saw you jump in. That was so funny!'*

But a couple of years ago, I was one of those people that did inch by inch...carefully...carefully...and my daughter would get cranky at me!

But right now, and for the last few years... I've been jumping right in! Is that what you're doing in life?

I wonder.

Changing course

Ok so everyone (I think) loves a new year/month/week/day!

But, I am wary of New Year's resolutions, in particular, that last just a month/week or even hours on some things.

You want to take your life in a different direction.
You want to take your health in a different direction.
You want to take your relationships in a different direction.
You want to take your career in a different direction.
Great. Well done for recognising you want to change something. But...

Here is the part that a lot of people get wrong.

They don't have a map/plan/strategy/clear outcome on how to do this.

They just give it a go like throwing shit at a wall and hoping it will stick. #sotrue

They change course and hope for the best.

If this isn't you, I congratulate you!

Think about a car journey across Australia. You don't just pull off Parramatta Road in Sydney and decide to travel across the country, do you?

Did you know the drive distance is the same as driving from London to Moscow?

Anyway, back to the point.

When you decide to make a long car trip - you make a plan.

You get a map. You talk to people (or research) other people who have made the same journey. You take tools in case you break down. You take fuel and food to use along the way. You get support by telling people where you are going. You also take a compass to use too.

Ok, let's use this example for a life-changing decision.

You decide to lose weight and increase your health. What is your plan? Where is your map? Who can help you do this, can you speak to people who have already done this? What tools will you use?

What fuel do you need? Who can support you along the way? Do you have a direction (compass)?

Let's break it down a bit more:

Losing Weight/Getting Healthier

* Plan - What do you want? How much do you want to lose? How will you do this? When will you do this by?

* Map - How will you get direction? Do you need someone to help you read the map? Do you need a PT or coach to help?

* Who do you know that has done this already? Talk to them, ask them how they did it. Ask them who helped them?

* Tools - use the internet/books/youtube vids to inspire you/ideas. Can you make a home-gym? Can you get some weights from Kmart and start with them? I am cautious of recommending gyms as they are not for everyone... but if you feel that is a good option - go for it. Does the gym have a PT? Can you attend local fitness groups?

* Fuel - this isn't just about food fuelling your body. It's about what drives you. Why are you doing this? WHY? This one is super important as if it's not strong enough, you won't achieve your goal.

* Support - get your whole families' support on this. There is no point on you eating salad when they get KFC every night and don't respect the choice you have made. Get a coach - they can help you mentally and keep you accountable (Yes I can help). Get a PT or share a PT for more accountability and new ideas.

Get online and tell people what you are doing for even MORE accountability.

* What's your direction?
* Where are you headed?

* Are you looking for a lifetime of health?
* Are you looking to do a marathon?
* Where are you headed and is that clear enough?

You can apply these types of questions to any area of your life!

Go for it.

I said nothing

So on some days, I struggle to find what to say on a blank piece of paper.

So I will keep typing till something comes up.

Hmmm...so nothing to say just yet.

Riiiight.

.

.

.

.

.

I suppose I can start with the fact that some of the conversations I have had over the last break with family/friends, I have had nothing to say back.

It's not them. It's me. I have changed.

I no longer talk about the past, hold grudges, gossip or blame others. It's not that that stuff didn't happen, or some people hurt me - but I find no need to talk/think about it. I see no point in wasting energy over the past. I no longer care about what other people are up to (unless it directly affects me in a danger sense).

I don't hold anyone else accountable for my life other than me. So I say nothing back, and I limit my time with them.

I can't contribute to the conversation anymore. I have nothing in common with them now.

And that's ok.

I still love them. I just don't enter into their realm and take part.

They say that if you still have the same friends you had five years ago, you haven't grown. That is true on my part. The mix of friends I have now is vastly different to 5 years ago. Don't get me wrong, I have a heap of mates from then (and further) I see still, but the immediate people in my life are only from the last couple of years or so.

Is this true for you?

I suppose in retrospect; this is all to do with learning and growing. I am a voracious learner, and I continually have my head in at least three books at a time. I also watch and listen to a lot of YouTube videos (Thank you YouTube Gods!) plus I attend seminars/workshops throughout the year to not only learn new shit but to network and make new friends.

It's kinda cool.

I wouldn't have it any other way.

So did I have nothing to say then? *Nope.*

I just needed to start. And that's the trick. People put off things, not knowing what to do... but if they just started something who knows what they could achieve? Not knowing what the outcome will be...not knowing where it will take them...not knowing what they will learn about themselves...

Just do something - then just see.

I can't get no satisfaction.

Actually, I don't even want it

I don't want satisfaction

Satisfaction.

What does this word mean to you?

Yes, it's a word, and it can mean so many things to different people.

I don't know about you - but I do not want satisfaction in my life.

No way! Not a chance. I do not want to be satisfied at all.

Why? Keep reading - or not. Especially if you are already satisfied with reading this far anyway.

Are you aiming for satisfaction in your life? Do you want satisfaction in your job or business? Are you happy with achieving satisfaction in your relationships? How satisfied are you with your health?

What are your thoughts? Are you satisfied with your goal/aim?

Being satisfied with your life = you are comfortable and perhaps have even sold out on life. No check that, you have sold out.

I am totally ok if you disagree with me too. I could be playing devil's advocate...

Being comfortable is easy. Being comfortable means, you don't push yourself. You have sold out on your potential.

Don't get me wrong! If you are ok with the comfy bit - stick with it. Don't listen to me. In fact, you probably don't even read books like this as they ask questions that make you a bit uncomfortable anyway.

'Oh but I don't know what to do!'
'Where do I start?'
'I want to still fit in with my family/friends.'

Piffle.

Start doing something. Stop caring about fitting in, yes you may get a bit of resistance, but that's normal as they don't want you to change as maybe you won't love them. Ever heard of the saying that a dog barks at things he doesn't understand? And no I am not calling your family dogs.

You have potential. Start recognising that.

You have control of the wheel.

Stop letting others take over from you - that's easy.

That's satisfaction.

What will you do today to change this?

I dare you to do nothing and wake up tomorrow/next week/next month/next year/next decade having taken the easy road.

Where will that get you?

Look at people who have stepped up and made the change. Copy what they did, ask them how they did it.

Follow in their footsteps and make a difference. Today.

Friendship Goals

So I know lots of people talk about goals in different areas of their lives - but have you ever had friendship goals?

As you know for some people (for me in particular as my family are in Old Blighty'), friends are super important. In fact sometimes more important than family.

But as we get older, our friendship circles can get smaller as people move away, have different/busy lives or people just come apart for no real reason. But hey! We still need friends, don't we?

Friends are a type of relationship. And relationships are important - why?

Relationships and friendships magnify the human experience.

Imagine going to the top of a mountain and looking at the view. Going on your own- how is that experience?

What about going there with someone else? Friend or partner? How much better is that? Your experience is magnified, yes?

Can you see what I mean by it magnifying our lives?

So back to friends.

So who are your friends and do they influence you?

Be honest too. Do you see them out of feeling guilt? Or do you see them because you genuinely want to hang out with them and you both give each other support, kindness, and love?

Evaluate the people surrounding you. Are they your Ra-Ra team (cheerleaders)?

Do they cheer you on or bring you down?

Do you find yourself comparing yourself to them and feeling bitter or disappointed?

Or do you have nothing in common anymore?

Do you feed off of each other and it's non-stop laughs?

It's a great idea to think about your peeps. If you have goals that your people are not going to support you on - find people who will!

They don't have to live near you either - you can find friends online and talk on the phone. Last year I met a few friends online (Facebook actually) and now we speak regularly and support each other via phone calls, emails, and SMS. I don't know what I would have done without them!

Again, back to you and your friendship goals.

What are they?

Who would you like to spend time with or connect with?

Do you know what your new friendships would look like?

What ways could you deepen your current friendships?

Food for thought I'm sure.

Push it.

Salt n' Pepa said it right.

You gotta push it. Push it REAL good.

insert hip thrusts

Push what?

Anything my friend. If you want to get somewhere - you gotta push.

I could stop there. But you have to start asking better questions, yes?

What is pushing? What is somewhere? Why do I have to push? What am I pushing?

Are you confused yet?

Good. It's working...

Get out of the 'settling' mindset.

Get out of the 'that will do' bull shit that you tell yourself.

Get out of the 'I'll get there one day/week/month/year/decade/lifetime' crap.

Get out of the excuses. The whiny voice in your head that says you can't do it.

Get out of the people around you telling you that you can't do it because it's too expensive/too risky/too easy/too much/too hard/insert another stupid excuse here.

Just push through all that. Push it real good.

Get clear on where you are headed. Set achievable goals. Have a bloody amazing reason why you are doing it.

Define what you are doing.

Then push.

Don't listen to yours or their voices.

JDFI.

Push it real good.

Don't stop believing

Don't stop believin' Hold on to that feelin'...

Gosh, that's a great song by Journey (1981) Check out YouTube, to listen to it if you can't remember what song I am talking about.

Anyhoo now that song is safely in your head for the next 24 hours - it makes sense doesn't it?

We **feel** things.

We are emotional creatures us humans, yes? Ok, some people act like robots, but I am talking about the majority here. (Especially women, right?)

We do things by how we feel. And sometimes we forget that.

We try to logic that 'feeling' into something else.

Ever done this? I know I have, countless times!

Why do we do it?

We have *forgotten*.

We have forgotten what it is to trust ourselves and our guts. Or our hearts.

We have forgotten to trust. We have forgotten that we know shit. You have forgotten.

But it's ok because you can remember.

It's in those times where we 'miss' something because we are so busy, rushing, focusing on something or someone else. Those moments that the wrong thing is said or done because we are worried about what someone will think.

Come back to you.

Come back to the simple things.

Breathe. Breathe. And breathe some more. Your body needs oxygen more than water, but you don't breathe enough.

Take 10 secs to breathe, take a moment and then speak/do/go.

Start with that.

You got this.

Listen here

When you talk to people do you really listen?

Be totally honest here.

I know people say they are good listeners but are they really?

When you listen, do you relate the topic to what you would do? What you would say? What you imagined to happen?

Do you reply with *'What I would have said is...'*? Do you respond in your head with that or similar?

Do you come back with something that has reminded you of something you had to mention/do/your experience/say?

Are you really listening?

I'd say not - if anything is coming to your mind about you.

Listening is about keeping an open mind, being present, being attentive and asking questions to get clarification. Hold the space for the person and be there with them. No judgment.

What it's not about is trying to 'fix' straight away - unless asked to of course.

Don't anticipate what they are going to say/do - based upon what they have previously done (there's judgment there) too.

Give them the space they need; they may come up with solutions by themselves.

Also, be empathetic - it takes energy and concentration, yes, but it's generous and helpful on your part.

Boys - women are talking to you to be heard. Not to be fixed.

Just listen.

I want to be heard

What is it about that makes us want to be 'heard?'

Why do you want to be heard?

I have a belief that it's similar to wanting to be in a relationship.

To somehow validate our lives, here on this planet. To confirm that we were 'something' and we had a witness to our life.

Deep? Perhaps? But certainly, something to consider...

Wanting to be heard is the same, that we are validated. That we are recognised as being something or someone. We are real; we have feelings and that we are important.

Being heard also means we are accepted.

Yes, all that caveman stuff still exists these days. Wanting to be part of the tribe and fitting in etc. If we are expelled from the tribe, we can die as we have no-one to protect us.

We still do it now, don't we?

I always giggle inside when I imagine the cavemen times - as so much of it still occurs. The picture in my head is that the men have beards and the women are wearing skimpy outfits or whatever. Kinda similar to today's famous people me thinks...

So, being heard. How can you do it?

It's simple. Either find someone who is a great listener or train your people to be great listeners. It's all down to communication.

Communicate to them that it's important to you, and what would be important to them? Perhaps they want to be heard too - but in a different way.

Another awesome way of being heard is by writing it all down. Journalling is a great tool to get all your shit out there. I usually journal for private, but you can let someone see it. It's up to you.

Get it all out on paper or blog it! It feels so good to write your shit out and get it outta your head.

Or maybe that's me.

But I believe that we are all similar in the end.

We are a simple species us humans...we are the same.

We want to be validated on this planet, and we love to talk about it.

Are you hearing me?

Stop your dreaming

'Get a proper job and do all that stuff after your kid has finished school.'

That's what they said to me. They told me to stop dreaming and get real.

Who are they? It doesn't matter really, does it? But yes they told me this. It felt like a blow to me; I physically hurt from those comments. I was in pain.

For a few days, I questioned everything I did. Then I realised. It wasn't about me. It was about them.

They weren't following their dreams, their ambitions, their true calling.

They were waiting until after the kids left school.

They were waiting for the right time.

Is there ever a right time for anything?

I believe there is time.

But if I waited for things to be perfect, nothing would happen. I would be a 'gunna.'

These days, I rarely hang out with gunna's. They don't upset or annoy me - I just know they are not ready and haven't realised their true potential yet. And that's ok.

Instead, I hang out with doers. Those people who aim for the stars and further...oh, and get their shit done and live.

It's pretty bloody fantastic. Each day is an opportunity. Each day something is learned. Each day is exciting. And if it isn't? That's ok too.

Dreams are a happening baby! Are Yours?

Cheering you

When was the last time you patted yourself on the back?

When was the last time you actually sat back and looked at what you have achieved?

I'll bet it's been a while...or ever?

Even for someone who works in the self-development field, even I forget to congratulate myself sometimes. Then I wonder why I feel flat and unmotivated.

I just don't think that we have been programmed to give ourselves pats on the back? And I know people are so into themselves that they forget to hi-five their family and friends.

What do you think?

So anyhoo - when I am feeling flat/low/unmotivated/uninspired I remind myself that I haven't recognised what I have achieved...then I do a mini-party for myself. Party pies included.

Jokes.

But I do a ritual of sorts.

I take time out (no more than 30 mins) and chuck some music on (music that makes me boogie) and write down the 25 things I have achieved in the last 12 months, or 6 months...whatever is needed.

Then I go through my diary or Facebook pictures to remind me of what I have done. I don't stop till I get to 25 things. THEN I CELEBRATE!!

How do I celebrate?

Do I get pissed? Not really...sometimes I will raise a glass to myself. But usually I will treat myself to something like a massage or a new book. Sometimes I have celebrated by taking myself away to Sydney for the night in a hotel for some peace and relaxation. But this type of thing doesn't have to cost money. You can easily celebrate your wins $ free. Go for a walk to a beautiful view and spend some alone time, or get back to nature. *Whatever floats your boat.*

But do **something.**

Recognise your wins.

Recognise your achievements.

Pat yourself on the back.

Then share the love by patting someone else on the back. :) Honestly - do this ritual at least once a month, pop a reminder in your diary if you need to. It feels amazeballs!

So what have you done recently, that you can cheer yourself on with?

If you can dream it - you can do it - Walt Disney

A poster of Cinderella caught my eye this today It got me thinking about good ol' Walt Disney. Bless his soul.

One of his sayings that I have in my kitchen, in the pic for this chapter - **If you can dream it, you can do it.** How cool is this?

And he is right.

Whatever you imagine to be, can be done. You just gotta open your mind to the possibilities.

And that is where I think we sell ourselves short. We restrict our dreams as 'impossible' or 'too far fetched'. We play small and don't want to stand out (too much).

Who's fault? Oh I could prattle on about your parents, their parents, the government, society...whatever. Who really gives a toss?

I know I no longer care.

I just know that I refuse to listen to the bullshit and I will dream about anything I wish.

Then I will take **action.**

I'll be honest though, I never actually dreamt that I would be doing this, because just a few years ago... I was working for the Government (worked there for 9 years) in a comfortable well paid easy-ish job. I had a heap of friends, social life and things were fairly 'easy'.

What changed? I listened to my heart. I 'knew' this wasn't the life for me. I had said from 18 years old that I wouldn't work in an office environment. Yet what did I do? Worked in an office from 19 - 33 years old.

Wow. It's interesting what we focus on...we do actually get. Even if it's the opposite of what we want!

I listened in.

I made a plan.

It felt right to study and learn.

So I did.

I studied for over 12 months and started working on my business even before I left my comfortable job. I transitioned out of it.

What did I also do...? I burnt my bridges. So I would have no way of going back. I had no plan B.

So I jumped.

I was so scared. I thought I would fall.

But I didn't.... I flew!

Over the last six or seven years I have fell hard heaps of times.

I have also flown **very high** heaps of times.

I wouldn't have it any other way. No more 'safe' for me.

No more control over what I do day to day.

Therein lies the magic. Dreams can happen, even when you don't know you have a dream. You just have to 'listen' to your heart and soul.

It knows the answers.

Then have faith...and breathe.

So my friend, what are you dreaming of?

Where's your choice?

So I reckon we have **choice** in life. For the majority of the time. *Now I am not talking about incidents out of our control*...like car accidents and other awful things like that.

I am talking about life choices.

Who we partner with or our friends. Our job or career. Our health. Our dreams.

We all have a choice in this.

I know some of you will say that you don't. But I want you to have an honest discussion with yourself about this.

Are you choosing to take part in X, Y or Z?
Are you choosing to blame another person or entity for your situation?

Are you choosing to remain unfulfilled because you feel like you don't deserve more?

Are you choosing to play small, to fit in with everyone else?

Are you choosing to remain with where you are because you feel guilty?

Are you choosing to not put yourself first because you don't have 'time' or another excuse?

What are you choosing in life? What could you do to change this?

I know from personal experience that being aware of your 'choices' is the first step.

Then taking responsibility is the second.

This one is massive and one that was very hard to swallow. It still is on occasion if I'm honest.

Taking responsibility for my reactions to things, to my feelings and my actions was big...like Tom Hanks **BIG.** A massive leap in my head for sure!

But **wowsers..!** It's so bloody refreshing!

What a feeling to know that you have control over your feelings?

What an amazing gift to find.

But hey! I am far from perfect. I still work on this stuff DAILY. But it's ok, because each day it gets better...and I am excited for the journey ahead.

Dearest reader,

Whether you get your shit done or not - is your choice.

You don't have to listen to me - *but I guess you read this book, so maybe you did?*

If you are keen to make more changes in your life, please do contact me. I am available for group coaching and I run a lot of programs regularly online.

But really, I'm just like you. I'm from a normal background and a bit had various shit happen in my life (like you, no doubt).

I believe in me, I believe in my message and I have faith that I can achieve every goal and dream I have.

Stay tuned for more awesomeness. Over and out.
Emma Queen
xx

Expert in getting shit done

Author, Mentor, Coach & Mum

www.emmaqueen.com.au

Connect with me on social media on the following channels:

www.facebook.com/expertingettingshitdone

www.instagram.com/emma_queen_australia

www.youtube.com/user/simplefitgong

https://au.linkedin.com/in/coachemma

The playlist to go with this book is under #getshitdone or type in the following URL:

http://spoti.fi/1QAX8De

My commitment:

I .... will get my shit done by
....

I will take action and JFDI.

Signed

....

Date

....

My commitment:

I .... will get my shit done by
....

I will take action and JFDI.

Signed

....

Date

....

www.ingramcontent.com/pod-product-compliance
Lightning Source LLC
Chambersburg PA
CBHW070424010526
44118CB00014B/1893